The best a statesman can do
is to listen to the footsteps of God,
get ahold of the hem of his cloak,
and walk with him a few steps of the way.

—OTTO VON BISMARCK

THE
RUMSFELD WAY

THE
RUMSFELD WAY

*Leadership Wisdom
of a Battle-Hardened
Maverick*

JEFFREY A. KRAMES

McGraw-Hill

New York Chicago San Francisco Lisbon
London Madrid Mexico City Milan New Delhi
San Juan Seoul Singapore Sydney Toronto

Property of Library
Cape Fear Comm College
Wilmington, N. C.

McGraw-Hill

A Division of The **McGraw-Hill** Companies

Copyright © 2002 by The **McGraw-Hill** Companies, Inc. All rights reserved. Printed in the United States of America. Except as permitted under the United States Copyright Act of 1976, no part of this publication may be reproduced or distributed in any form or by any means, or stored in a data base or retrieval system, without the prior written permission of the publisher.

1 2 3 4 5 6 7 8 9 0 AGM/AGM 0 9 8 7 6 5 4 3 2

ISBN 0-07-140641-7

Cataloguing in publication data is on file for this title at the Library of Congress.

Printed and bound by Quebecor World, Martinsburg.

FIRST EDITION

McGraw-Hill books are available at special quantity discounts to use as premiums and sales promotions, or for use in corporate training programs. For more information, please write to the Director of Special Sales, Professional Publishing, McGraw-Hill, Two Penn Plaza, New York, NY 10121-2298. Or contact your local bookstore.

♲ This book is printed on recycled, acid-free paper containing a minimum of 50% recycled, de-inked fiber.

The Rumsfeld Way is not authorized, endorsed by or affiliated with Donald Rumsfeld.

To Nancy,
for her significant contributions to this work,
and for her far more profound
contributions
to my life

CONTENTS

THE
RUMSFELD WAY

RUMSFELD'S RETURN

AUGUST 9, 1974: It would be a day like no other in American history. In a one-sentence letter written in the Lincoln Sitting Room in the White House, Richard Nixon resigned the presidency of the United States.

Vice President Gerald Ford, who awoke early that morning, climbed into a limousine for his fateful trip into Washington. Once he had settled in, he was handed a four-page memo outlining the decisions he would need to make soon after being sworn in as America's thirty-eighth president. "We share your view that there should be no chief of staff," the document read in part, reflecting an opinion Ford had expressed previously. "However, there should be someone who could rapidly and efficiently organize the new staff, but who will not be perceived or be eager to be chief of staff."

Ford, well aware of history bearing down upon him, reflected once again upon this critical decision. Unexpectedly, the former congressman found himself presiding over one of the darkest moments in the nation's history. This was not the time for bickering or infighting. Ford knew he needed someone strong enough to ride herd on the situation without appearing overly aggressive or ambitious. His transition team—already in disarray—had recommended Frank Carlucci, the highly regarded former HEW secretary. There were two other alternatives, including

1

Deputy Defense Secretary William P. Clements, Jr. But as the limo glided over the bridge that separated Virginia from the nation's capital, Ford wrote the name of the man who would be charged with handling one of the most difficult transfers of power in America's history:

RUMSFELD

Friday, January 11, 2002, the Pentagon, 2:10 P.M. EST: More than eighty reporters have already jockeyed for their plywood seats as nearly a million viewers tune in, awaiting the beginning of the latest best show on earth: the "Rummy Show." At least twice a week, and often more frequently, the sixty-nine-year-old, bespectacled secretary of defense, Donald H. Rumsfeld, has hosted a briefing to deliver the latest news on the war against terrorism. Indisputably, he has become the face and voice of the war. His prickly yet candid answers to often repetitive questions have won over, even mesmerized, a historically skeptical Washington press corps.

In the days before the briefing, there had been disturbing press reports that a certain number of high-ranking Taliban and al Qaeda personnel had been captured and—for reasons yet unknown—released. If this were true, it would represent an embarrassing situation for the U.S. government, which was committed to holding and interrogating any such prisoners. The exchange that followed captures the quintessential Rumsfeld and goes some way toward explaining the unlikely popularity of the Rummy Show:

> Q: *Mr. Secretary.... What's your reaction to the release of seven Taliban leaders in Kandahar, and some of them senior?*
>
> RUMSFELD: *I've read those reports and I've tracked them down two days in a row, and we can't verify*

that that ever happened, that there were ever those people in custody, that anyone—it's hard to be released if you were never in custody.

Q: *So you're saying it didn't happen?*

RUMSFELD: *I'm not saying it didn't happen.*

Q: *Oh.*

RUMSFELD: *I'm saying precisely what I said.*

Q: *Okay.*

RUMSFELD: *That for two days, I've tried to track down these fascinating stories I've been reading in the press and hearing debated on television, and I am not able to do so....I keep pursuing it and saying, "My goodness. They can't all be wrong. Please see if you can't find what they're writing about." But I can't find what people have been writing about and talking about on television. I can't find it. But this does not say it didn't happen.*

A question or two later, while other reporters are clamoring to be recognized, Rumsfeld thinks of one more thing to add to that discussion, and goes back to it:

Q: *Mr. Secretary—*

Q: *Mr. Secretary—*

RUMSFELD: *Wait a second. If there's anyone in this room who can give me any more information about these people who were supposed to be in custody, whether you've written about it or not—(laughter)—I'll be available after the meeting.*

That's a typical Rumsfeld exchange. The subject could hardly be more serious, yet Rumsfeld attacks it with a hard-nosed humor. And despite his obvious lack of awe for the media, he has developed a rapport with the press seldom seen in the post-Watergate era. One reason is that he shows them a different kind of respect. He is not afraid to say that he doesn't have every answer. He also announces straight out when he doesn't want to talk about something. And because he is careful not to pass on any information that is not verified, he is generally taken at his word by both the press and the public.

Absent the events of September 11th, the Rumsfeld phenomenon would not have been born, and the Rumsfeld story might never have been written. But in the wake of the terrorist tragedy and Rumsfeld's response to it, the complete Rumsfeld record—a four decade career in private and public life—warranted a thorough examination.

What emerged was a portrait of a *leader*. No, Rumsfeld has not always been "perfect"—far from it—but his record of accomplishment is considerable. And it seemed that the lessons he points us toward, implicitly and explicitly, could be applied in a great variety of situations, both inside and outside of the world of business.

What follows are the leadership lessons learned by a man who twice has been called upon to manage and lead during times of great uncertainty, and who has altered the destiny of the nation in two separate presidential administrations, some three decades apart.

EVOLUTION OF A STATESMAN

1

THE ROAD TO KANDAHAR

I think he [Rumsfeld] is one of
the seminal figures of this period.

—HENRY KISSINGER, FEBRUARY 2002

*All eyes are on the straight-shooting former
navy pilot who is running the war.*

—NEWSWEEK ON DONALD RUMSFELD

HE HAS BEEN DUBBED "the Articulator in Chief of this perilous effort" by the *Washington Post*, and CNN called him "the media star of America's new war." CNN's Bernard Kalb said, "The press corps had surrendered to Rummy," despite frustration with the scant amount of information he was providing. Conservative commentator George Will praised to the rooftops his "damn the torpedoes, full speed ahead" approach to the war. Even the boss was taking note. Upon signing the defense appropriations bill early in 2002, President Bush kidded Rumsfeld on his unexpected celebrity. "I always love being introduced by a matinee television idol," Bush quipped.

And even the *New York Times* commented on Rumsfeld's celebrity. In a tongue-in-cheek piece in early December 2001, columnist Maureen Dowd declared Rumsfeld to be the ringleader of a new Rat Pack, likening him to the original Rat Pack's "chairman of the board," Frank Sinatra: "Forget about Clooney and Pitt mimicking vintage testosterone in the new Rat Pack remake. We've got the real deal right here...the suave swagger of Rummy and Cheney enhanced by cluster bombs and secure locations instead of martinis and broads. Who needs the men of "Oceans 11" when you've got the men of September 11?"

Not that the new Chairman of the Board is a pub-crawler. Far from it, in fact. Away from the glare of the briefing or television interview spotlights, and of course excepting official trips, a public Rumsfeld sighting is a rare event indeed. He is seldom seen out on the town, far preferring the quiet and privacy of his Pentagon office, with its windows tinted yellow to deter electronic surveillance.

When he *did* venture out into society in early 2002, it was to attend the Washington premier of *Black Hawk Down*. (This was, apparently, only the second movie Rumsfeld attended in years. The only other was *Saving Private Ryan*.) Judging by the paparazzi who greeted him and the press coverage that followed the event, this was less like a Washington cabinet member venturing out in public and more like an appearance by a movie star.

Even Rumsfeld, who prides himself on his ability to spin scenarios and look into the future, has been caught off guard by his star status. But the lapse is certainly forgivable. In fact, in a culture in which youth and beauty reign supreme, who could have predicted that this unlikely, aging figure—old enough to be the grandfather of some current pop idols—would capture the imagination of the nation. When was the last time *curmudgeonly* was hip?

But the rules that applied to the United States before September 11th no longer pertain. In the wake of the nation's terrible tragedy, Americans looked for someone with gravitas, someone who had a firm hand on the tiller. And as if on cue, there on CNN, dead serious but never self-important, was Secretary of Defense Donald H. Rumsfeld.

THE RIGHT MAN AT THE RIGHT TIME

During his first few months on the job, Rumsfeld spent much of his time talking about missile defense and a makeover for the military. Despite the promise of the most rigorous and far-reaching overhaul of the military in history, however, most Americans took little notice of him. Some in the press—when they paid attention to Rumsfeld at all—depicted him as an aging politician out of touch with the new ways of Washington. Others saw him as an ultra-conservative "Darth Vader" type who would pursue missile and space defense at the expense of other more pressing programs. By early September, there were even murmurs of an "early exit" for "Rummy" (including a September 7th *Washington Post* story that speculated about who might replace him).

But from the first moments following the attacks, Rumsfeld emerged as a compelling figure. Flanked by the chairman of the Joint Chiefs of Staff, General Hugh Shelton (as well as two U.S. senators), in a building that was still burning, Rumsfeld struck a note of grief, calm, and purpose. "This is a tragic day for our country," he said. "Our hearts and prayers go to the injured, their families, and friends. We have taken a series of measures to prevent further attacks and to determine who is responsible. We're making every effort to take care of the injured and the casualties in the building."

The Bush administration made a particular point of stressing *continuity* amid seeming chaos. "The United States government is functioning in the face of this terrible act against our country," Rumsfeld said. "I should add that the briefing here is taking place in the Pentagon. The Pentagon's functioning. It will be in business tomorrow."

By the following day, the government was moving from reaction to action, and Rumsfeld played his part in this transition. He subtly de-emphasized damage assessment and began outlining the Bush administration's plan for moving forward. He introduced Americans to the concept of "a new twenty-first-century battlefield." By all accounts, he excelled in the immediate wake of the attacks, emerging as a cantankerous but capable leader at a point when America badly needed direction.

What struck many observers most forcefully was Rumsfeld's acid-tongued candor. Truth-telling, especially with a hard edge, seems strangely out of place when it emerges from the defense establishment. We have become all too accustomed to our military brass (and their civilian counterparts) describing war in euphemisms and sanitized phrases. By departing so forcefully from that tradition, Rumsfeld has etched himself a sharp profile in our minds. Yes, he's sometimes prickly and acerbic, but he's also oddly refreshing and reassuring.

Rumsfeld finds himself in the final act of a four-decade-long career. Today, he appears to have no qualms about setting an errant journalist straight. If he doesn't know something, he doesn't hesitate to say so. If he doesn't want to answer a certain question, he says that too: "Those aren't the kinds of things one discusses," or "It's not the time for discussions like that." And on the flip side, he may choose to respond to a question with an almost alarming directness. At one press conference, Rumsfeld was asked why U.S. warplanes were bombing in a certain area. "To kill them [al Qaeda and Taliban fighters]," he replied. In another meeting with the press, he used the word "kill" nine times—probably an all-time record for a Pentagon press briefing. As the *Economist* put it, "Mr. Rumsfeld's waffle quotient is remarkably low: he either speaks straightforwardly, or not at all."

So he possesses the gift of candor—a no-nonsense direct-ness so notable that it achieved the pop-culture status of getting spoofed on "Saturday Night Live" in late 2001. At the same time, he draws upon a store of earthy, pungent images and metaphors, often with quirky or colorful expressions. The result can be striking. When asked if the United States was close to apprehending fugitive terrorists in Afghanistan (Osama bin Laden), he replied, "If you're chasing a chicken around the barnyard, are you close or are you not close until you get him?"

Journalist and pundit Walter Lippmann observed the ways of power in Washington for many years. "Successful politicians are insecure and intimidated men, who advance politically only as they placate, appease, bribe, seduce, bamboozle, or otherwise manage to manipulate the news," he once observed. "Politics has become one of our most neglected, our most abused, and our most ignored professions."

Most modern administrations have only compounded the problem. The Johnson administration obfuscated its way through Vietnam. ("Why should Ho Chi Minh believe me," Johnson complained, "when the newspapers and broadcasters in my own country won't believe me?") Richard Nixon was elected in part because he had a "secret plan" to end the Vietnam War—which he turned out not to have—and eventually got caught in his own Watergate snares.

Gerald Ford pardoned Nixon, and never recovered from that act. Jimmy Carter was squeaky clean but deemed ineffective. Even Ronald Reagan—the so-called Teflon president—was held accountable for the Iran-Contra scandal. The first George Bush was punished for flip-flopping on a tax increase—and Bill Clinton, of course, wounded himself mortally with the Lewinsky affair.

In the early days of 2002, it is apparent that people trust President Bush, Vice President Richard B. Cheney, and Secretary of State Colin Powell. For the first time in decades, in fact, a broad cross section of America has confidence in its leaders. Most Americans today would not agree with journalist Lippmann's assessment that politicians advance as they "bamboozle" or "manipulate the news." Polls taken since the September 11th attacks suggest that more than two-thirds of Americans trust their government, a figure not approached since America's victory in the Gulf War.

And Donald Rumsfeld is one of the reasons for this important sea change. In the days and weeks following September 11th, it became increasingly clear that Donald Rumsfeld was the right man in the right job at the right time. Those close to him insist that he hasn't changed. Perhaps he hasn't—but the world clearly has. And in the new world that emerged in the wake of September 11th, a long-time master of the Washington power game finally found himself in circumstances that would catapult him onto the world stage, like no other event in his already distinguished career.

The secretary of defense's own words, delivered to members of the U.S. Armed Forces twenty-four hours after the attack, suggest that he, too, felt that he was ready for the challenge. By invoking the words of Churchill to the U.S. Armed Forces, Rumsfeld was, in essence, throwing down the gauntlet, asking the men and women in the service to rise to the occasion as their predecessors had in World War II:

> *Great crises are marked by their memorable*
> *moments. At the height of peril to his own nation,*
> *Winston Churchill spoke of their finest hour.*
> *Yesterday, America and the cause of human freedom*
> *came under attack, and the great crisis of America's*
> *twenty-first century was suddenly upon us.*

Some might have blinked at the approach of the hand of destiny. Rumsfeld did not. What explains his "state of readiness" in the post–September 11th world? First, his many years of maneuvering in the minefields of Washington politics had rendered him one of Washington's most experienced political infighters. But just as important, Rumsfeld had unparalleled experience managing complex situations in times of national crisis and uncertainty. The most vivid example of this was Rumsfeld's management of the post-Watergate Ford White House, at a time when the executive branch found itself in a state of turmoil, even chaos.

MANAGING UNDER FIRE

Days prior to Nixon's resignation, the *Washington Post* ran a story entitled "A Capital in Agony." That headline summed up the feelings of a dazed electorate, who had watched the unfortunate events of Watergate play out over many months. In two centuries of American history, no sitting president had been forced from office except at the ballot box. Now the nation was embarking on uncharted waters, and it was indeed a time of "agony"—not just for Washington, but for the American people.

While the aftermaths of Watergate and September 11th were enormously different, there are some obvious parallels as well. Both crises created great uncertainty—a sense that the nation was at great risk if it stood still and yet had no clear path forward. In the wake of Nixon's resignation, Americans felt that their political process, even their democracy, had been violated. It was no accident that Gerald Ford titled his memoir *A Time to Heal*.

The tragic events of September 11th, too, created a sense of violation. Beyond inflicting staggering costs and catastrophic loss of life in New York, Washington, and Pennsylvania, the attacks cast a deep shadow on the national spirit. Most Americans felt that the enemy "was among us" and feared other attacks were imminent. The majority of Americans suddenly felt unsafe doing things that they had done routinely for decades, such as flying on commercial aircraft and working in tall buildings. It seemed impossible that normalcy could be restored, that Americans could ever feel as safe as they had prior to September 11th, or that they would ever again enjoy the luxury of doing "business as usual."

While the entire Bush team rose to this great challenge (e.g., Dick Cheney and Colin Powell), it was Donald Rumsfeld who had the unique role of reassuring the American people and keeping the nation informed on the progress of the war against terrorism. Although there were other seasoned and articulate cabinet members whom Bush could have selected for this critical role—both Secretary of State Powell and Vice President Cheney had served as highly effective spokespeople during Desert Storm, for example—Rumsfeld was designated the voice of the war, and the voice of reassurance, by the Bush administration.

There is one more unavoidable parallel between Watergate and September 11th. In recent years, national crises have become a collective experience shared in real time, mainly through the ubiquitous presence of TV. "We're all Watergate junkies," one observer confessed during that time of crisis. "Some of us are mainlining, some are sniffing...but we are all addicted." The same could be said for September 11th and the war on terrorism, only this time the addiction was even more widespread. In the intervening quarter-century, cable television had insinuated itself into America's living rooms and bedrooms. (By 2000, more than 80 percent of American households were either cable or satellite subscribers.) This meant that twenty-four-hour-a-day news services like MSNBC were available to satisfy our cravings for the latest news from Afghanistan (CNN even aired a weeknight show entitled "Live from Afghanistan").

And for the most part, it was Rumsfeld that CNN and its competitors served up to us, day after day. Not surprisingly, millions of Americans were soon asking the obvious questions: *Who is this Donald Rumsfeld? And where on earth did he come from?*

RUMSFELD: WHO AND WHY?

The strength that matters most is not the
strength of arms, but the strength of character;
character expressed in service to
something larger than ourselves.

—DONALD RUMSFELD, FEBRUARY 2001

The worst day of his tenure has proved to be the best for his professional fortunes. It's transformed the beleaguered Pentagon chief into the smash success of the administration's war on terrorism, and afforded him a brand new start.

—BALTIMORE SUN

IN THIS CHAPTER, we will ask and answer the question posed by millions of TV viewers in recent months: Who is Donald Rumsfeld?

In the process, we'll also answer a related question: *Why a leadership book based on his experiences and observations?*

A point to stress: This book is not a biography of Donald Rumsfeld. The biographical material that follows is intended to give the reader a context for the second part of this book, which examines Rumsfeld's career thematically. But because we will soon abandon chronology, it makes sense to include a timeline of Rumsfeld's life and career to date, and to discuss some highlights from that chronology.

FROM WINNETKA TO WASHINGTON

Born in the Chicago suburbs in 1932, Donald Rumsfeld was the son of a Chicago real estate man. He won a scholarship to Princeton and emerged as the captain of both the football and the wrestling team. Legend has it that Rumsfeld the collegian—already emerging as a tough character—would do one-armed push-ups for money. When asked why years later (by NBC's Tim Russert), Rumsfeld recalled that he "didn't have much money and needed to scrape together a few [dollars]."

A RUMSFELD CHRONOLOGY

July 9, 1932	Born in Chicago, Illinois, son of George Donald Rumsfeld and Jeannette R. (Huster) Rumsfeld
1954	Princeton University scholarship student (awarded A.B. degree in 1954)
Dec. 27, 1954	Married Joyce Pierson
1954	Began three years of service in the U.S. Navy as a Naval aviator
1957–1958	Administrative Assistant, U.S. Congress
1959	Staff Assistant, U.S. Congress
1960–1962	Representative at the Chicago investment banking firm A. G. Becker and Company
1963	Elected to the U.S. House of Representatives from Illinois; reelected in 1964, 1966, and 1968
1969	Resigned from Congress during his fourth term to join the Nixon Administration
1969–1970	Served in the Nixon Administration as director of the Office of Economic Opportunity, assistant to the president, and member of the president's cabinet
1971–1972	Counselor to the president, director of the Economic Stabilization Program, and member of the president's cabinet
1973–1974	U.S. ambassador to the North Atlantic Treaty Organization in Brussels, Belgium
1974	Returned to Washington in August to join the Ford administration as chairman of the transition to the presidency of Gerald R. Ford
1974–1975	Chief of staff of the White House and member of the president's cabinet

Nov. 11, 1975	Appointment as U.S. secretary of defense confirmed by the Senate
Nov. 20, 1975	Took office as thirteenth U.S. secretary of defense, the youngest in U.S. history
Jan. 20, 1977	Left office as U.S. secretary of defense with the change of presidential administrations
1977	Awarded the Presidential Medal of Freedom, the nation's highest civilian award
1977–1985	Chief executive officer and president of G. D. Searle & Co., a multinational pharmaceutical company
June 1, 1985	Chairman of the board of Searle, the first in the company's history not a member of the Searle family
1982–1986	Member of the president's General Advisory Committee on Arms Control in the Reagan administration
1982–1983	President Reagan's special envoy on the Law of the Sea Treaty
1983–1984	President Reagan's special envoy to the Middle East
1983–1984	Senior advisor to President Reagan's Panel on Strategic Systems
1983–1984	Member of the U.S. Joint Advisory Commission on U.S.-Japan Relations in the Reagan administration
May 30, 1986	*Wall Street Journal* announces that Rumsfeld to seek GOP nomination (for presidency in 1988 election).
March 2, 1987	Announced he would not run for president of the United States
1987–1990	Member of the National Commission on the Public Service

continued on next page

A RUMSFELD CHRONOLOGY

1988–1989	Member of the National Economic Commission
1988–1992	Member of the Board of Visitors of the National Defense University
1989–1991	Member of the Commission on U.S.-Japan Relations
1990–1993	Chairman and chief executive officer of General Instrument Corporation
1992–1993	Member of the U.S. Federal Communication Commission's High Definition Television Advisory Committee
1993–1998	Worked in private business and also maintained alliances with several Republican causes/commissions
1996	Helped handle Bob Dole's presidential campaign against incumbent Bill Clinton.
1998–1999	Chairman, Commission to Assess the Ballistic Missile Threat to the United States (became known as the "Rumsfeld Commission").
1999–2000	Member of the U.S. Trade Deficit Review Commission
2000	Chairman of the Commission to Assess United States National Security Space Management and Organization.
Jan. 20, 2001	Confirmed as secretary of defense in the administration of George W. Bush

Sources: http://www.defenselink.mil/bios/secdef_bio.html; David B. Sicilia and Robert Sobel, eds., *Biographical Directory of the United States Executive Branch, 1774-2001* (Westport, Conn.: Greenwood, 2002).

In 1954—the year he married—Rumsfeld graduated from Princeton with a major in politics. In preparation for a military career, he joined the Navy as an aviator. (Following the rigorous path he had already staked out at Princeton, Rumsfeld grappled his way to becoming All Navy Wrestling Champion.) But after dipping his toe into the water of politics on the staff of an Ohio representative, the twenty-nine-year-old Rumsfeld ran for Congress from the thirteenth District in Illinois. The Rumsfeld campaign was dominated by young and enthusiastic volunteers, with Rumsfeld himself "exuding a style suggestive of a conservative Kennedy." He won the first of four terms in the U.S. Congress by almost a two-to-one margin.

Rumsfeld's congressional voting record turned out to be an apt predictor of his lifelong political habits. In most realms, he was consistently conservative, earning him a 100 percent ("perfect") rating from the conservative Americans for Constitutional Action. The liberal Americans for Democratic Action, conversely, gave him a 4 percent rating.

His strong right-wing tendencies were moderated, however, by his stalwart support for civil rights and by his willingness to take on and reform the old Republican guard. One Rumsfeld move that particularly irked conservatives and alienated the far right was his role in helping to take the House minority leadership role away from Charles W. Halleck and give it to Gerald Ford. The right-wing hostility resulting from this power play was a significant factor in helping Rumsfeld lose his bid to chair the House Republican Research Committee in 1969. Rumsfeld's career, now stalled, needed something to spark it back to life. This was when Richard Nixon entered the picture.

OUT OF THE WATERGATE LOOP

Nixon—himself a pragmatic conservative—was impressed enough by the four-term congressman that he asked him to head the Office of Economic Opportunity (OEO) in 1969. One of the chief tasks of the OEO in the Nixon era was to "de-escalate the war on poverty" declared by the Johnson administration. In taking the post, Rumsfeld became a director of a government agency with a high profile. Still, Rumsfeld's decision to take the job (which most thought to be a bureaucratic nightmare) surprised many of his colleagues on Capitol Hill, including Gerald Ford. Rumsfeld felt that the agency "ought to be kept around if for no other reason than...to maintain at least one credible national symbol and program which demonstrates our Government's commitment to the poor."

Rumsfeld vowed to transform the OEO from an "activist agency" to an "initiating agency." During his nineteen-month stint at the OEO, Rumsfeld did in fact streamline the agency to some extent, forcing it to become more efficient and more focused on teamwork. But the real surprise came when Rumsfeld began to make active and energetic efforts to keep the OEO's poverty programs alive rather than dismantling them outright.

This won him enemies on the Republican right, who felt that their old friend Rummy had "gone liberal." Critics blamed him for giving in to political pressures from Nixon's inner circle. After all, he had been a conservative, pro-business congressman. Most observers believed that under Rumsfeld, the OEO would be killed. Instead, he made it more consistent with the policies and philosophies of the Nixon administration.

Happy with Rumsfeld's performance, Nixon rewarded him with several additional positions in the ensuing four years. Rumsfeld turned down Nixon's offer of the GOP chairmanship, and, instead, Nixon appointed him counselor to the president in 1970. Next came the directorship of the Cost of Living Council (CLC); in this position Rumsfeld administered Nixon's price and wage controls.

Rumsfeld's Council duties brought him onto the Domestic Council, where he butted heads with notorious Nixon aides H. R. Haldeman and John Ehrlichman. Somewhere during this period, Rumsfeld's political "gut" kicked in. Sensing that he needed to distance himself from both the CLC and the Nixon White House, Rumsfeld got himself nominated as ambassador to NATO in 1972. One of the storm signals on the horizon that Rumsfeld may have sensed was the worsening economic picture: by taking the NATO post in December of 1972, he was long gone from the CLC when prices began to skyrocket.

As a result, the perceptive Rumsfeld was thousands of miles from the U.S. when the first Watergate-related stories started to surface in the *Washington Post*. According to Nixon (as he relayed it in his memoir, *RN*), the ever-loyal Rumsfeld did offer to resign his NATO position in late June "to help work against impeachment among his former colleagues in Congress." For whatever reason, that offer didn't amount to anything, and Rumsfeld retained his NATO post until after Nixon resigned in August.

This helps to explain why Rumsfeld was not considered "damaged goods" in the wake of Watergate. From the outset, some of Ford's advisors worried about Nixon holdovers who kept their key positions after Nixon's departure. But since their days in Congress together, Ford always had been fond of his friend Rummy, and he thought that no one was better qualified to spearhead the difficult transition.

FORD'S RIGHT ARM

In his memoir, Rumsfeld's old boss, President Ford, was generous with praise for his onetime chief of staff. "The fact that he [Rumsfeld] was in the Nixon White House from the earliest days and didn't get involved in Watergate," Ford wrote, "said much about his personal integrity." In discussing Rumsfeld's strengths, he also provided an explanation of why the Watergate participants did not risk Rumsfeld's involvement: "He wouldn't tolerate political shenanigans and the men around Nixon knew he wouldn't, so to protect themselves, they kept him out of the loop."

Within hours of Nixon's resignation, Ford asked Rumsfeld to spearhead a five-person task force that would help to get Ford's White House in order. Rumsfeld agreed, and he quickly learned of the extent of Ford's problems. After making his suggestions to Ford, Rumsfeld returned to Brussels to resume his NATO duties. That was when things in the Ford White House went from bad to worse.

In September, Ford made the fateful decision that would damage his authority and impair his ability to govern. After "agonizing" over the decision for weeks, he pardoned Richard Nixon, feeling it was the best thing he could do to begin to heal a tormented nation. After the announcement, Ford's approval rating plummeted from 71 percent to 49 percent, with many Americans concluding that Nixon and Ford had struck some sort of dirty deal. According to Ford's memoir, he simply failed to anticipate "the vehemence of the hostile reaction to my decision." Some of Nixon's critics apparently wanted to see him drawn and quartered. Once again, however, while most of this was playing out, Rumsfeld was in Europe, far away from the stench of the decision.

However, Rumsfeld returned to Illinois in late September of 1974 in order to attend his father's funeral. That's when

Ford summoned him back to Washington. (At the same time, Ford arranged for Alexander Haig, who had been operating as Ford's chief of staff, to take the position of NATO commander, thus clearing the field.) Ford knew he needed a decisive chief of staff and begged Rumsfeld to take the job. Initially Rumsfeld said no, but then he reluctantly agreed.

How Rumsfeld would manage and organize the Ford White House became the subject of intense speculation, and Ford insiders subsequently devoted a lot of space in their memoirs to the subject. In retrospect, many concluded that Rumsfeld outmaneuvered everyone, including the formidable Henry Kissinger, in amassing more personal power than any other member of the cabinet. (Exactly how he accomplished this is the subject of several chapters in this book.) Although Rumsfeld served as Ford's chief of staff for just over twelve months (from October 1974 to October 1975), his time in that position tells us much about Donald Rumsfeld and his ability to wield power and influence and manage a particularly turbulent White House.

THE HALLOWEEN MASSACRE

By the fall of 1975, Ford was unhappy with the state of affairs in the White House and felt that it was time to do some shaking up of his own. In particular, he had become convinced that he had not been aggressive enough in removing Nixon holdovers. During the Halloween weekend, therefore, Ford set in motion a sweeping plan to reshuffle his cabinet. Because of the timing of his reorganization and the drastic nature of the changes, the Ford plan became known as the "Halloween Massacre." The plan was disclosed on November 1, 1975, but actually had been in the works for some time.

Disillusioned with his secretary of defense, James Schlesinger, Ford decided in October to fire him. But that was only the beginning. Henry Kissinger, who had been wearing two hats as both Secretary of State and National Security Advisor, was stripped of his NSA responsibilities. William Colby, who headed a beleaguered CIA (then being investigated for illegal surveillance), was fired too (Colby was fired because conservatives felt he had exposed the agency to far too much public scrutiny). Also "pink-slipped" was Vice President Rockefeller, who reluctantly agreed to remove himself from the 1976 ticket. Ford's motive in making these potentially divisive changes was to close ranks with the Republican right in order to increase his chances for reelection in 1976.

The decisions that Ford made that fall did little to help his reelection bid and far more to ignite controversy and embitter many of the participants for years to come. In fact, according to journalist John Osborne, the prominent journalist who covered the White House for the *New Republic*, Ford's moves prompted "hatred"—a word that Osborne said he was fully justified in using based on his conversations with the key participants. And much of the hatred was aimed at one individual in particular: Donald Rumsfeld.

Rumsfeld quickly acquired a reputation as a cold-blooded back-room operator. Most observers therefore concluded that Rumsfeld was behind Ford's most objectionable decisions. That interpretation is understandable, since the Halloween Massacre both reflected and enhanced Rumsfeld's enormous power. He wound up as Secretary of Defense, and Rumsfeld's protégé, Dick Cheney, succeeded Rumsfeld as Ford's chief of staff.

Meanwhile, George Herbert Walker Bush became director of the CIA. This appointment in particular deserves some scrutiny. Bush was then the U.S. ambassador to China and had hopes of being a vice presidential contender in 1976. In response to the offer of the CIA directorship—a post that he eventually accepted—Bush fired off an angry telegram to Ford. "I do not have politics out of my system entirely," he growled, "and I see this as a total end of any political future." Insiders speculated that Rumsfeld was behind the decision to dispatch Bush to the CIA—as well as the previous decision to remove Rockefeller from the ticket. With Rockefeller and Bush out of contention, Rumsfeld's path to the vice presidency was now cleared.

The *perception* that the Halloween Massacre reflected a bagful of "Rummy maneuvers" wound up costing Rumsfeld dearly. Almost overnight, he accumulated a constellation of powerful enemies—enough, in fact, that his political prospects apparently dimmed to the point of disappearing.

Ironically, at least some of the allegations of devious dealings by Rumsfeld appear to have been a bum rap. Early in 2002, *Esquire* ran a story that shed new light on the events surrounding the Halloween Massacre. The article's author, Wil Hylton, located a July 10, 1975, Rumsfeld memorandum marked "Administratively Confidential, Memorandum for the President" in the bowels of the Gerald R. Ford library in Ann Arbor, Michigan. In that memo, Rumsfeld suggested ten potential replacements for William Colby at CIA. *Not* on the list was George Bush. So unless the memo provided cover for some as yet undiscovered deeper plot, Rumsfeld was not guilty of exiling Bush to the CIA.

In assuming the Pentagon post, Rumsfeld—then age forty-three—became the youngest secretary of defense in history. Despite his impressive resume, which included his NATO experience, Rumsfeld's appointment ignited more

controversy. Many felt that Rumsfeld's cabinet appointment was bringing a partisan neophyte into the administration. Others felt that Rumsfeld had bigger things in
mind for his future than a Ford cabinet post. None of this
criticism prevented his swift confirmation, however.

During his tenure of fourteen months (between 1975
and 1977), Rumsfeld argued for increases in defense spending. One of his primary goals was to ensure that the U.S.
was ready to engage the Soviet Union in war, should it ever
come to that. In his 1977 annual report, Rumsfeld included the following statement: "U.S. strategic forces retain a
substantial credible capability to deter an all-out nuclear
attack." Still, Rumsfeld was able to spearhead the development of certain advanced weapon systems, including the B-
1 bomber, the Trident nuclear submarine program, and the
MX ICBM. His greatest coup, however, may have been the
championing of a new weapon called the cruise missile (the
same weapon that later played such important roles in the
Gulf War and in NATO's Kosovo campaign).

Rumsfeld was able to do this while contending with
some of the stickiest issues of the cold war. For example,
Rumsfeld, who believed more in defense than in détente
with the Soviet Union, avoided the risky position of sup-
porting the second round of the Strategic Arms Limitations
Talks (SALT II). Instead, he simply followed a "stall and
harass" strategy, which had the effect of killing the treaty.

William Hyland, editor of *Foreign Affairs*, felt that
Rumsfeld was thinking of his own political career when it
came to SALT II, which was regarded as a compromise
treaty and too controversial to support. Rumsfeld was perhaps the most important member of the hawkish contin-
gency in the Ford Administration who harbored serious
doubts about the SALT II Treaty. The fact that a staunch
anti-Communist, Ronald Reagan, had made such a serious

run for the Republican nomination against Ford only empowered this group of advisors. The internal leverage from the hawks and the external leverage of the conservative Reagan candidacy were instrumental in obstructing progress on the Treaty.

Others saw Rumsfeld's tactics in undermining SALT II as more evidence of the Machiavellian politician who would do most anything to advance his own agenda. Ford later admitted that there was little hope of getting SALT II signed given the stance the defense department had adopted. According to William Hyland, (Jimmy) Carter's campaign staff's "greatest fear" for the 1976 election was that Ford would indeed announce a SALT agreement in the fall. Of course, it was not to be.

FROM PENTAGON CHIEF TO CEO

After leaving government following Ford's defeat in 1976, Rumsfeld put in a brief stint in academia, lecturing at both Princeton and Northwestern. He then accepted an offer to join G. D. Searle, an Illinois-based pharmaceutical company that had contributed to Rumsfeld's political campaigns, as that company's chief executive officer.

By almost any measure, it was an astounding offer. A family-run corporation for decades, Searle was then in trouble, sinking under the weight of its increasing size and the lack of a clear strategy and agenda. To most observers, Rumsfeld—who had never run anything other than a congressional campaign—seemed like a truly awful choice. What was needed, many felt, was an experienced manager who understood the intricacies of running a large corporation.

Rumsfeld, for his part, was the first to admit that, with the minor exception of having been a stockbroker before becoming a congressman, he had absolutely no private sector experience. Now he was coming in at the top of a substantial corporation. But he possessed an extraordinary degree of self-confidence, apparently because he believed that the skills he had acquired in government would serve him well in his new position:

> *What I learned about crisis management and troubleshooting in the Nixon and Ford Administrations helped make the government-to-industry transition easier. I found the change from Congress to the executive branch harder to make than from the executive branch to business.*

Inside the company, too, people had their misgivings— which in some sense proved justified. Rumsfeld was known as an "axman," and he soon made good on that reputation, firing more than half of the corporate staff. By all accounts, he was merciless in trimming what he perceived to be deadwood. According to the *New York Times*, he fired some people by calling them at home, or even paging them at airports.

But as it turned out, Rumsfeld was an excellent choice for Searle. During his eight-year stint at the helm of the pharmaceutical maker, he helped turn the company's fortunes around in dramatic fashion. He did so by "streamlining" operations (a standard Rumsfeld move), getting costs in line, and selling off non-drug businesses. The turnaround at Searle earned him back-to-back awards as Outstanding Chief Executive Officer in the pharmaceutical business in 1980 and 1981. Under his leadership, Searle's stock price soared by a factor of five.

During his tenure at Searle, Rumsfeld's greatest challenge involved gaining government approval of the most important product in the company's history, the artificial sweetener aspartame (later branded as NutraSweet). After years of going head-to-head with Washington regulators, he and a colleague at Searle did something that virtually everyone they consulted told them *not* to do: They sued the FDA for approval of aspartame. Soon after, the product was approved and went on to become a huge hit. With that win behind him, Rumsfeld then arranged the sale of the company to chemical industry giant Monsanto, personally netting more than eight figures in the transaction.

THE ROAD BACK

Following his retirement from Searle in 1985, Rumsfeld kept a foot in the private sector, serving as head of two more companies over the ensuing fifteen years. He also continued to accept the string of public service posts that began coming to him in the early Reagan years. He served, for example, as senior advisor to President Reagan's Panel on Strategic Systems and as Reagan's envoy both on the Law of the Sea Treaty and to the Middle East, and later served as a member of the National Commission on the Public Service.

Rumsfeld briefly considered a White House run of his own for the 1988 election. Although the bid fizzled quickly, some pundits, including conservative commentator George Will, were thrilled at the thought of a Rumsfeld White House. Will praised the former congressman for "the hardness in his gaze and temperament" and also dubbed him a "Republican heartthrob" to succeed Ronald Reagan. When Rumsfeld pulled out of the race, he backed underdog Bob Dole rather than the favorite, George Herbert Walker Bush.

In March of 1988, after Texas senator John Tower's embarrassing failure to be confirmed as secretary of defense, the *Wall Street Journal* took a highly unusual step.

Although the paper declared, "it is not the habit of this newspaper to endorse named individuals for specific posts," the *Journal* called for the assignment of Rumsfeld as secretary of defense. "We think that of all the names in speculation for the appointment, one stands out above all in fulfilling the criteria....Former Defense Secretary Donald Rumsfeld is the obvious choice." It is a small irony of history that Rumsfeld would indeed become defense secretary in the Bush Administration—although the appointment did not become a reality for another decade and he wound up serving the son rather than the father.

In 1996, Dole—heading back out on the campaign trail, this time as the Republicans' presidential nominee—asked Rumsfeld to become policy coordinator for his campaign. Dole, not the soul of discipline or organization, apparently figured that he could benefit from Rumsfeld's managerial experience and efficiency. According to Bob Woodward's book *The Choice*, Rumsfeld was near the top of Dole's list for vice president that same year. Eventually, though, he chose former football star and congressman Jack Kemp as his running mate.

Rumsfeld, for his part, was keenly aware that Dole was a long shot against Bill Clinton but was convinced by conservative friends to take on Dole's cause. In managing the campaign, he persuaded Dole to promise massive tax cuts and take a more hard-line approach on defense issues. With prodding from Rumsfeld, Dole attacked Clinton for his managing of Iraq and also advocated the deployment of a national missile shield by 2003. According to the *Nation*, these moves helped to lay the foundation for George W. Bush's campaign against Vice President Al Gore in 2000. (Unfortunately for Dole, Rumsfeld's tactics did nothing to help his chances, as the GOP had largely abandoned Dole a month before the campaign.)

After the 1996 election, Rumsfeld made one more detour into the world of business, taking over a biotechnology company called Gilead Sciences. He also served on the boards of several high-profile companies, including the Tribune Company and European electrical giant Asea Brown Boveri. Throughout this period, though, Rumsfeld continued to cultivate his ties to the conservative community, most notably through his association with a think tank called the Center for Security Policy. That organization, founded by a former Reagan official, was set up to campaign for the deployment of "Star Wars" defenses.

Thanks to Rumsfeld's noteworthy resume, his Republican ties, and honed management skills, in 1998 he was asked to chair the Commission to Assess the Ballistic Missile Threat to the United States. This commission became known as "the Rumsfeld commission," and its primary purpose was to review classified intelligence information on the ballistic missile programs of such "rogue nations" as Iraq, Iran, and North Korea in order to assess their future ability to attack the United States. The commission determined that one or more of these nations might be able to deploy missiles capable of hitting the United States within five years, or one-third the time then estimated by the CIA.

The work of the commission may help explain why, in December 1998, Rumsfeld (along with his protégé Paul Wolfowitz, R. James Woolsey, and others) sent a letter to President Clinton asking his administration for "a strategy for removing Saddam's [Hussein] regime from power. This will require a full complement of diplomatic, political, and military efforts," declared the document.

In January of 2001, Rumsfeld released the findings of another commission that he chaired. Called the Commission to Assess United States National Security Space Management and Organization (dubbed the "Space Commission," or

Rumsfeld II), it reached conclusions even more controversial than those of the 1998 Rumsfeld commission (Rumsfeld I), although it received far less attention. The Space Commission warned of a "space Pearl Harbor," in which hostile countries could attack American satellites in space, thus hampering America's ability to function. As a result, the Commission unanimously agreed that the United States had "an urgent interest in promoting and protecting the peaceful use of space." This meant, somewhat paradoxically, that Rumsfeld would argue for "the weaponization of space, sooner rather than later."

MEETING THE "THREATS OF A NEW CENTURY"

Although many regarded Rumsfeld's views on missile defense and the weaponization of space as extreme, it became apparent that they fit the Bush agenda as outlined in his presidential campaign. It is worth noting, however, that Rumsfeld was not Bush's first choice to head the Pentagon. Rumsfeld's selection as secretary of defense came after President-elect Bush had already interviewed former Senator Dan Coats of Indiana, whom many expected would be named to the post (another name that had surfaced as a candidate was Paul Wolfowitz, who would go on to become Rumsfeld's deputy secretary). Ultimately, it appears likely that Bush went with his vice president's choice, Dick Cheney's old friend and mentor, Donald Rumsfeld.

However, Bush was well aware of Rumsfeld's stance on missile defense, having been briefed by Rumsfeld in May of 1999. After the meeting, Bush had remarked that Rumsfeld had reinforced his thinking on the subject. Bush incorporated several of the Rumsfeld themes into his own campaign, including a promise to develop new high tech weapons, a hard line position on Iraq and other "rogue nations," and a sweeping transformation of U.S. military policy. Bush cited these topics in a speech he delivered at the Citadel in September of 1999.

When President-elect Bush announced that Rumsfeld would be his choice for secretary of defense in late December of 2000, he once again echoed many of Rumsfeld's ideas and conveyed his support for a strategic transformation of the military: "We must work to change our military to meet the threats of a new century. And so one of Secretary Rumsfeld's first tasks will be to challenge the status quo within the Pentagon, to develop a strategy necessary to have a force equipped for warfare of the twenty-first century."

In his turn at the microphone, Rumsfeld declared that he would undertake a massive refurbishment of military policy in order to prepare the military for what he viewed as a new model of warfare, made necessary by the post-cold war reality in which the greatest threats emanated from rogue nations with unconventional weapons: "It is clearly not a time at the Pentagon for presiding or calibrating modestly. Rather, we are in a new national security environment. We do need to be arranged to deal with the new threats, not the old ones."

Rumsfeld had been speaking of these new perils for years, and many observers felt that the Rumsfeld appointment signaled a far more aggressive U.S. military policy, one more likely to alienate even some U.S. allies. Military expert Michael Klare, for example, writing in the *Nation* in January of 2001, declared that "...there is no doubt that Bush and Rumsfeld will push much harder for deployment of a national missile shield and for the deployment of weapons in space. They are also likely to abandon the ABM treaty, which prohibits missile defenses of the sort they favor."

"CARPET-BOMBING" AND
"THE MYTH OF THE SUPER-CEO"?

For compelling evidence of how dramatically the events of September 11th turned the world upside down, one need only look at the press coverage of Donald Rumsfeld in the weeks leading up to the disaster. Several articles were highly critical of Rumsfeld, characterizing him as an out-of-touch bureaucrat. In August and early September of 2001, *Business Week*, *Newsweek*, and *Time* all ran stories that outlined the failings of what most deemed to be a relic of a bygone era.

Business Week (which, in the spirit of full disclosure, is owned by the McGraw-Hill Companies, which also employs this author) may have been the source of the most merciless coverage of Rumsfeld. In a piece entitled "Why the Hawks Are Carpet-Bombing Rumsfeld," the article speculated on reasons for Rumsfeld's apparent decline:

> *The ex-CEO of G. D. Searle & Co. had bold plans to build a high-tech military, push a missile defense system, and cut costs. But all he has done so far is alienate the military brass, defense industry execs, and Congress. While jabs from the left were predictable, what's surprising is the thunder on the right—including one leading conservative's suggestion that he resign.*

The piece quoted one senior GOP congressional aide who declared, "There is almost nobody in this town who is not tearing him to pieces." The article also noted that William Kristol, editor of the *Weekly Standard*, "called on Rumsfeld to resign to highlight 'the impending evisceration of the American military.'"

Newsweek's story, entitled "The Myth of the Super-CEO," claimed that "Rumsfeld and [Treasury Secretary

Paul] O'Neill are the latest chiefs to fumble in a place where power works differently." The piece stated that both were foundering in their jobs and that "Rumsfeld and O'Neill are not doing badly *despite* having been successful CEOs but *because* of it."

The article suggested that Rumsfeld's ways no longer worked in Washington, where power "is diffuse and horizontally spread out." The article also suggested that former CEO Rumsfeld would not have the patience to listen or learn, suffering from what one senior executive calls "the Sun King syndrome"—an "ailment" brought on when someone bathes in the spotlight of "adoration" and "sycophancy" too long.

Time, in its August 27th story entitled "Rumsfeld: Older, but Wiser?," suggested that the defense secretary made several major missteps in his first months in the job. He excluded key top officials from his decision making, instead going outside the military to get advice. (Excluding top brass from meetings is a common criticism of Rumsfeld, especially inside the Pentagon.)

When rumors of Rumsfeld's plan to close military bases surfaced, this angered many in the Pentagon, who secretly started to work against him (reactivating an anti-Clinton faction that formed inside the Pentagon when Clinton announced his intention to loosen rules against gays in the military). This meant that Rumsfeld's efforts were being "thwarted" by Pentagon insiders, according to *Time*. The magazine quoted a senior Pentagon official who explained how insiders were working against Rumsfeld: "What the uniformed guys put in place to undermine the last President was now being used to undermine Rummy."

The tragic events of September 11th forever altered the political calculus in Washington and New York. With the possible exceptions of President Bush and Mayor Rudolph Giuliani of New York, no other politician's fortunes were so dramatically reversed in the wake of September 11th. This doesn't mean, of course, that the previous criticisms of Rumsfeld were without merit. He has admitted that it took him some time to adjust to the new rules of Washington and that he could have handled some things better. (He also claims to have been shocked by how quickly information is leaked out of today's Pentagon, exclaiming that all he has to do is *think* of something and it gets out.)

But his ability to improvise so effectively since September 11th suggests that the media (and just about everyone else) underestimated Rumsfeld. Beneath the overly familiar surface of a man his critics perceived as being out of touch with the new ways of Washington was a battle-hardened leader who possessed one of the most crucial of leadership qualities: an adaptive reflex that kicked into gear when it was needed most. From the first moments of the crisis, a resolute and capable leader emerged, quickly erasing the doubts and whispers that had filled newspapers, magazines, and Washington corridors in the preceding weeks.

INTERPRETING RUMSFELD

Despite Donald Rumsfeld's lengthy resume in both government and industry, relatively little has been written about him, particularly in comparison with other contemporary figures. No biographer seems to have taken on Rumsfeld as a subject, for example, and few encyclopedias contain even a single "Rumsfeld" entry.

Rumsfeld *does*, however, turn up in the pages of other people's memoirs, including those of Henry Kissinger and Gerald Ford. These reminiscences, when combined with his speeches, articles, interviews, and government documents, help to shed insight into the complex figure that is Donald Rumsfeld (and proved invaluable in writing this book).

To interpret Rumsfeld, one can also turn to *Rumsfeld's Rules*, a brief manual that Rumsfeld wrote in the late 1970s and which he has revised through the years. (The last revision, by chance, was made on September 10, 2001.) *The New Republic* proclaims the short manual to be probably Rumsfeld's "most notable political legacy." The text includes more than 100 nuggets on what to do—and not to do—while serving in the political and business arenas. One "Rumsfeld Rule," for example, reads as follows:

> *Plan backwards as well as forward. Set objectives*
> *and trace back to see how to achieve them.*
> *You may find that no path can get you there.*
> *Plan forward to see where your steps will take you,*
> *which may not be clear or intuitive.*

In 1988, the *New York Times* felt *Rumsfeld's Rules* important enough to run a feature story about them. Entitled "Rumsfeld's Rules of Ego," the article listed about a dozen of them. Pointedly, it also proclaimed, *Rumsfeld's Rules* can be profitably read in any organization. The article made a point of saying how valuable those rules are in the White House, "where humility does not easily flower." In 2001, the *Wall Street Journal* featured *Rumsfeld's Rules* in a front-page story and reported that they had been downloaded from the Internet more than 50,000 times (by 2002, in light of Rumsfeld's popularity, and the fact that they are sometimes mentioned at Rumsfeld's briefings, that number likely increased many times over).

One of the most surprising aspects of the portrait of Rumsfeld that emerges as one reviews the written record is how many feathers he has managed to ruffle throughout his career. As noted above, Rumsfeld's political maneuverings have made him many an enemy. Over the years he has feuded with such noteworthy figures as Henry Kissinger, Brent Scowcroft, and Nelson Rockefeller, although few of these individuals spoke on the record of their true feelings. In fact, public statements have often masked the intense feelings that some have felt toward him.

For example, in his memoir, Henry Kissinger called Rumsfeld a "skilled full-time politician-bureaucrat in whom ambition, ability, and substance fuse seamlessly." But in private, Kissinger did describe Rumsfeld as ruthless. It should be noted, however, that Kissinger does not feel that ruthlessness is necessarily incompatible with being a great statesman. In an interview in early 2002, Kissinger explained that frictions were inevitable in light of the fact that he had been a cabinet member for eight years and Rumsfeld was a relative newcomer. "There is an inevitable conflict in an election year on issues…between the secretary of defense and secretary of state," he notes.

The individual who was perhaps the most outspoken on Rumsfeld was Nixon aide and Watergate participant Bob Haldeman. In his diary, he described an incident in which Rumsfeld misled the Nixon staff in pursuit of a job. Haldeman called it "typical Rumsfeld" and a "rather slimy maneuver." That's the bluntest of the Rumsfeld rebukes one can find and—considering its source—a rather troubling one.

By all accounts, Rumsfeld has been brusque and aggressive. He has also been *persistent*. Rumsfeld has the rare distinction of being the youngest—and the oldest—individual to occupy the office of secretary of defense, as well as the only person ever to hold the job twice. It should not be surprising that Rumsfeld's ways tormented many. After all, one does not often achieve high posts without being a shrewd back-room operator. Ford speechwriter Hartmann once summed up Rumsfeld as being "ruthless within the rules."

So, "ruthless," yes. But this, too, is overly simplistic. There is ample evidence that Rumsfeld is a fair-minded, decisive, and responsible leader with significant talents, and an almost instinctual sense for survival in the very different worlds of politics and business. And although few today remember Rumsfeld's accomplishments in the private sector, it's fair to say that his business career was particularly impressive. Arthur M. Wood, a former chairman of Sears and a Searle director, called him "tough-minded." John Robson, long-time ally and the attorney whom Rumsfeld hired at Searle, said, "Don is a gifted leader with executive instincts and executive talent that has manifested itself wherever he's been."

In a cover story on Treasury Secretary Paul O'Neill in the *New York Times Magazine* in early 2002, author Michael Lewis asserted, "If you asked a seriously competent CEO...whom in the Bush administration he admires as a businessperson, the only name he would come up with would be O'Neill's. Only O'Neill made his money by transforming a business and making it more productive."

Not only does that last statement slight the Rumsfeld record, it seems incorrect. Although at Searle, Rumsfeld operated on a far smaller scale than did O'Neill at Alcoa, Rumsfeld inherited an ailing company that had a troubled reputation in Washington, a failed diversification program, an inadequate research and development pipeline, and a weak management team. By the time he left Searle, all of these ills had been cured and the company's fortunes had been reversed.

In some ways, Rumsfeld's management tactics were ahead of their time. For example, Rumsfeld demanded that his organizations become lean and decentralized and that they not let bureaucracy interfere with their performance. He exhorted his managers to "know your customers" and readily fired people who couldn't perform to his standards. To some extent, he therefore begs comparison with other CEOs who would later emerge as celebrities.

For example, Jack Welch, the acclaimed former CEO of General Electric, was dubbed "Neutron Jack" for massive downsizings of his company in the mid-1980s. He also spent years at the helm of GE streamlining the corporation, removing management layers, arguing for decentralization and firing nonperformers. Rumsfeld employed some of these same management tactics earlier than Welch, but on a far smaller scale, and not under the same spotlight afforded one of the world's premier corporations.

Finally, it should be noted that Rumsfeld is an extremely rare commodity in having climbed to the top of both the political and the business hierarchies, and achieved outstanding success in both arenas. This reflects skill and persistence. But it also reflects luck. Rumsfeld has always had an uncanny knack for being in the right place at the right time, and for being away from "the wrong spot at the right time." Watergate was only the most obvious example. There have been many others.

A TALE OF TWO RUMSFELDS

One of the most compelling parts of the "Rumsfeld as leader" story is that over the years, there appears to have been *two* Rumsfelds. That is not to say that America's twenty-first secretary of defense has undergone some dramatic transformation in recent years. He is still the same hard-charging leader who goes to work at 6:30 A.M., puts in fourteen-hour days, sends memos by the handful, often works standing up, makes unprepared underlings tremble, and never loses sight of the mission at hand. That's classic Donald Rumsfeld.

But the Rumsfeld of today—the secretary of defense who quotes Winston Churchill and speaks of preserving the American way of life—seems to be in many ways a more *evolved* figure than the one who operated in the Ford White House and ran G. D. Searle with an iron fist. The "early" Rumsfeld (the congressman, Ford chief of staff, etc.) often seemed to have multiple agendas. His tactics and methods in that era suggested that ambition often trumped principle and that—like any skilled chess player—he spent inordinate amounts of time figuring out his next, better move. Rumsfeld's calculating mind enabled him to stay one step ahead of his foes, and his keen knowledge base on defense issues was one of his primary weapons.

However, later, a Midwestern genuineness shattered the otherwise acerbic demeanor, revealing a reflective wisdom that could only have been born out of many years of experience in both public and private life. The "straight-shooting" Midwesterner is the one that America saw most often in the aftermath of September 11th.

Henry Kissinger agrees with this assessment. In early 2002, he offered his own interpretation of "the two Rumsfelds:" "I think we're dealing with Rumsfeld now at a different stage of his life. In the 70s he was at the beginning of his political career. Now he is beyond further ambition. But I thought he was a formidable man then, and he's an outstanding leader now…The Rumsfeld of 2002 is concerned with public service and nothing else."

One of the reasons he has won such praise as secretary of defense (in his second tour) is that he seems to know himself—who he is and what he wants to do. Rumsfeld seems single-minded in his goal: to help end terrorism and make the world a safer place. In short, today's Rumsfeld seems far more comfortable in his own skin than his "predecessor."

Today's self-actualized Rumsfeld also has the benefit of a key asset that may have escaped others in his position: a keen grasp of and empathy for the accumulated lessons of history (right up to the Gulf War). One source that Rumsfeld has turned to in formulating his approach to the war on terrorism is the groundbreaking 1997 book by H. R. McMaster, *Dereliction of Duty: Lyndon Johnson, Robert McNamara, The Joint Chiefs of Staff, and the Lies that Led to Vietnam.* McMaster examines the decisions made in Washington between November of 1963 and July of 1965, and concludes that "the greatest foreign policy disaster of the twentieth century" was the result of "human failures at the highest levels of the U.S. government."

According to one insider, Rumsfeld was shocked at the level of deceit and manipulation that characterized America's handling of the Vietnam War, in which 50,000 Americans and uncounted Vietnamese, Cambodians, and Laotians lost their lives. This may explain why, in his briefings, Rumsfeld takes care not to mislead, and why he has erred on the side of silence rather than risk misleading or promising something that may be revealed to be untrue later. Around all Rumsfeld's cantankerousness, there seems to be an individual who is simultaneously passionate and compassionate as he tackles the enormous task at hand.

J. F. Clarke once declared that "a politician thinks of the next election; a statesman, of the next generation." The Rumsfeld of the Ford years was a politician (evidently with few equals). The Rumsfeld who emerged in the wake of September 11th is a statesman.

Winston Churchill once proclaimed that "responsibility is the price of greatness." During World War II, he also declared, "This is no time for ease or comfort. It is the time to dare and endure." Although Rumsfeld has been mistakenly labeled a "holdover"—and more than once—it is apparent that Rumsfeld has grasped the responsibility of the moment and understands how the current conflict differs from all previous wars. "What we are engaged in is something very, very different from World War II, Korea, Vietnam, the Gulf War, Kosovo, or Bosnia," Rumsfeld declared in September. Within hours of the terrorist attacks, it became apparent that the depth of Rumsfeld's experience would emerge as one of the great assets in the Bush administration's war on terrorism.

LESSONS FROM A HARD-CHARGING CEO

MISSION FIRST

The Urgency Imperative

If you get the objectives right,

even a lieutenant can write the strategy.

—FROM RUMSFELD'S RULES,

ATTRIBUTED TO GENERAL GEORGE MARSHALL

He is the kind of person who relishes a clear mission. A number of people were put off early on by the same attributes that are now gaining him so much applause.

—ANDREW KREPINEVICH, EXECUTIVE DIRECTOR

OF THE CENTER FOR STRATEGIC AND

BUDGETARY ASSESSMENTS, ON DONALD RUMSFELD

THE RUMSFELD RECORD REVEALS a leader who has both a keen sense of urgency and an instinct for quickly getting to the heart of a problem—both hallmarks of effective leadership. These qualities may sound like obvious virtues, but the fact is that many leaders take too much time identifying the problem and outlining possible responses. Those moments of hesitation can mean the difference between success and failure.

In late 2001, in the context of waging the war on terrorism, Rumsfeld spoke of the roles of "mission" and "task," and specifically on the importance of a *tightly defined* mission:

Once you allow the coalition to
determine the mission, whatever you do
gets watered down and inhibited so narrowly
that you can't really accomplish, you run the
risk of not being able to accomplish, those things
that you really must accomplish.

"The task overrides everything," Rumsfeld asserts, again stressing the importance of a clear problem definition. Throughout his years in both government and business, Rumsfeld's ability to define a situation and establish priorities, and to do so *quickly*, has helped him to succeed in particularly difficult situations.

SIDELINING HAIG

Rumsfeld has long understood the importance of setting priorities. In the first days of the new Ford administration, the newly appointed White House "chief" demonstrated both his mission focus and his sense of urgency—at a time when other members of the newly organized cabinet were either jockeying for position or still staggered by Nixon's resignation.

Once Rumsfeld agreed to take the top staff post—which was initially labeled "coordinator," rather than chief of staff, to head off any allegations of power-grabbing by Rumsfeld—he immersed himself in the job completely. When Ford initially met with his new transition team, the newly minted president had few concrete ideas of what he wanted the team to do, or even about how to organize the staff.

In that meeting, Ford "rambled" on about the transition. Perhaps sensing an opportunity, the ever-assertive Al Haig attempted to bolster his power base, suggesting that all cabinet members continue to report to *him* (Haig had been serving as temporary chief of staff). Earlier, Haig had said privately that he could "run [the] White House with the back of my hand."

Rumsfeld took everything in, speaking only rarely. He took careful notes on the challenges that faced the new and hastily constructed cabinet. In other words, while others were blustering, Rumsfeld was *listening*. In his *Rules* writings, Rumsfeld quotes R. Barr of St. John's College in Annapolis, Maryland to sum up his own feelings on the importance of listening:

> *The art of listening is indispensable for the right use of mind. It is also the most gracious, the most open, and the most generous of human habits.*

In this case, however, Rumsfeld wasn't necessarily listening for the sake of graciousness or generosity. He was searching for a definition of the new administration's top priority—a search that could only be aided by listening to others' views on mission. Here is how he wound up summarizing Ford's top mission: "To move from an illegitimate government in the minds of the American people to a legitimate government."

As it turned out, that clear mission statement was exactly what Ford and, by extension, the country needed. While Haig was consumed with trying to hang on to the power he had wielded under Nixon, Rumsfeld's notes suggest that he knew that there was a mission that was larger than either Haig or himself. That mission was to establish Gerald Ford as the rightful president of the United States. At that chaotic moment in the nation's history, nothing else mattered.

SUCCESS DEPENDS ON EXECUTION

As noted in previous chapters, Rumsfeld took over the ailing pharmaceutical maker G. D. Searle in the spring of 1977. The company, which started out as a small family-run pharmaceutical firm, had grown into a large multinational, involved in dozens of businesses around the world. Nevertheless, it was still being run like a small company, and the results were predictable. By the time Rumsfeld took over, the company had racked up eight losing quarters in a row.

In other words, the company had "outgrown" itself. It had gone on a buying spree starting in the 1960s and now had its hands in too many pies. This problem was exacerbated by a lack of clear and focused leadership. Instead of being led by a single chief executive officer, the company had a three-headed "committee" (two Searles and a brother-in-law) at its helm. Because decision-making was inevitably a group affair, the triumvirate structure bogged down the company and made it difficult for it to act decisively.

Tough decisions needed to be made—but they were unlikely to be made by Searle family members, who lacked the detachment and objectivity of an outsider. Although Rumsfeld had no formal background running a company, it didn't take the congressman-turned-CEO long to figure out what needed to be done: Size up the problem, pick the course of action, and *act*. Years later, he expressed his views on the importance of stepping back from a problem in order to take a more proactive position:

> *When you're dealing with the immediate all the time,*
> *you have to kind of just force yourself to step back*
> *and look at issues like those that are not the kinds of*
> *things that are going to end up in your in-box. No*
> *one's going to ask you those questions. They don't*
> *come at you, they've got to come out of you.*

When he was asked about the similarities between managing in government versus business, he spoke of the importance of priorities: "[Another] similarity in business and government is the need to establish priorities—to make sure you're spending time on what's important."

Years before other CEOs would win accolades for fixing troubled businesses, Rumsfeld demonstrated his instinct for getting right to the heart of the problem. In fact, although he didn't start at Searle until June of 1977, he had spent the previous three months talking to key insiders to determine what his opening moves would be.

Rumsfeld has been quoted as being an avid believer in what would become known as "participative management." He said he could not just bark out orders and expect the organization to follow them. Rumsfeld knew that the best way to turn the organization around was to set a decisive course, gain consensus from key players, and make sure the mission was properly executed:

> *In business, although it is more responsive than government, things don't just happen by command....It is helpful if employees understand what the direction is and why. To a great extent success will depend on their execution.*

Those who worked under Rumsfeld over the years might be surprised by this particular Rumsfeld pronouncement. At both Searle and the Pentagon, many inside and outside of those organizations felt that he had ruled with an iron fist, moved too aggressively, and didn't involve key personnel. But this may be a matter of *degree* more than of substance. The *Fortune* quote (above) makes clear that Rumsfeld was focused on success—and that he understood that getting people on board with the mission was a critical building block in that effort. And Rumsfeld, the pragmatist, was quick to deal with anything he believed to be at odds with his stated objectives.

"RUMSFELD'S SNOWFLAKES"

One of the tools that Rumsfeld used in articulating the mission and establishing company priorities was the liberal use of memos. Rumsfeld saw an opportunity to set the agenda with his communiqués and—conversely—not to let distractions rule the day. His torrent of memos became so infamous at both NATO and the Pentagon that they were actually given nicknames. At NATO, they were dubbed "yellow perils," because they were written on yellow paper. At the Pentagon, which stocked white paper, the memos became known as "Rumsfeld's snowflakes."

His memo-writing at Searle apparently never earned a nickname, but his pen was nevertheless busy during his tenure with that company. The drastic actions he undertook there—cutting costs, reducing head count, and aggressively bringing in new blood—were unlike any the company had ever seen. One key hire was John Robson, whom Rumsfeld had known and trusted since high school, as executive vice president of planning and regulatory affairs. Searle had had significant problems with the FDA over the years and needed someone to orchestrate its complex relationship with the agency. Robson became Rumsfeld's "point man" in this relationship and the key figure in his inner circle.

Rumsfeld next revitalized the research department, in part by bringing in a new senior vice president for research and development. He also initiated a licensing and acquisition strategy for the company's remaining businesses. Rumsfeld, who often purposely downplays his own accomplishments, described the turnaround of Searle this way:

What we did, essentially, was tidy up some of the pieces that didn't seem to be suitable platforms for growth. I enjoy working with talented people, learning from them, and arranging them in a way that they can be more productive.

But "tidy up the pieces" grossly understates Rumsfeld's far-ranging interventions at Searle. The record speaks for itself. After eight straight quarters of decline, Rumsfeld's Searle enjoyed five consecutive quarters of growth within his first two years at the helm. The turnaround was dramatic and indisputable, and ensured Rumsfeld's personal financial well-being. Under his leadership, as noted, Searle's stock price skyrocketed some 500 percent.

DEFINING "A NEW BATTLEFIELD"

Twenty-four hours after the horrific September 11th attacks on the World Trade Center and the Pentagon, Rumsfeld was still honing his own role and response. The nation was reeling. The last time a foreign nation had attacked Americans on U.S. soil had been six decades earlier, at Pearl Harbor—and that was a military action, not purposefully aimed at civilians. In his first formal briefing following the attack, Rumsfeld knew that he needed to provide a new *context* for what had occurred. Nothing remotely similar ever had taken place in the lives of most U.S. citizens, and the American people needed to be prepared for what might lie ahead.

After expressing his sympathy to the families, friends, and colleagues who had "been harmed," Rumsfeld moved to help people understand the nation's true circumstances in the wake of the tragic events:

> *We are, in a sense, seeing the definition of a new battlefield in the world, a twenty-first-century battlefield. And it is a different kind of conflict, it is something that is not unique to this century, to be sure, but it is—given our circumstance—it is in a major sense new for this country.*

Rumsfeld's carefully chosen words—"a twenty-first-century battlefield"—provided a context that people could understand. In the immediate wake of the attacks, many Americans felt frightened, depressed, or hopeless. By employing the term "battlefield," Rumsfeld was making the unfamiliar familiar. He was emphasizing that the administration viewed the terrorists' acts as *acts of war.* America would not sit back passively, as a victim, and allow other such acts to take place. Rumsfeld's words were no magic bullet—it still would take months for America to emerge from its state of shock—but he had laid a valuable foundation for recovery. He had used *mission* to reassure and galvanize the American people, initiating their healing process and firming their resolve.

How did Rumsfeld come up with the right words at the right time? Although he certainly had access to the best speechwriters, it appears that the Rumsfeld many of us were watching or listening to on September 12th was the real Rumsfeld—live, unrehearsed, and extraordinarily effective. And he was effective in large part because of the depth of his experience, honed over four decades of private and public service that thoroughly prepared him for this moment. That preparation was both general and specific. In numerous speeches, and also in at least one private conversation with President Bush earlier in the year, Rumsfeld had articulated his fears of an attack against America by a rogue nation.

Unfortunately, he was right. Fortunately, being right prepared him for the worst.

THE RUMSFELD WAY

Never underestimate the importance of listening: Remember that the "art of listening is indispensable." Effective leaders listen before they act. Rumsfeld says he likes to engage his brain before his mouth.

Look at your business/situation with a fresh eye: Start with a blank page. One of the reasons Rumsfeld was able to turn around Searle (and later a second company, General Instrument Corporation) was that he was able to evaluate the situation with an outsider's objectivity. Once you get locked into a particular set of actions or decisions, it may hamper your ability to change directions when the circumstances demand such a change.

Define the problem/situation: Immediately following the September 11th attacks, Rumsfeld defined the nature of the situation for a stunned nation. In doing so, he gave Americans a context for the horrific acts—and made it clear that the United States would not sit idly by as acts of evil were being committed on our shores.

Articulate a vision: Once he had defined the new battlefield, Rumsfeld made it clear that implementing the vision involved eradicating terrorist networks in Afghanistan and other nations around the world. He repeated this "mission statement" at every opportunity. In fact, like almost every effective leader, he never stopped articulating both the vision and the mission. This built support for the war both at home and abroad.

Don't coast; there isn't a moment to lose: Act quickly and decisively. Assume that if you don't, a competitor will. *Rumsfeld's Rules* quotes L. W. Pierson as saying, "If you're coasting, you're going downhill."

STRAIGHT TALK

Communicating Like a Leader

You will receive only honest, direct answers from me, and they'll either be that I know and I'll answer you, or I don't know, or I know and I won't answer you—that'll be it.

—DONALD RUMSFELD IN A DOD BRIEFING

The press briefings conducted by Secretary of Defense Donald Rumsfeld became a TV series, too, and 'fans' tuned in loyally. Rumsfeld appears in these sessions to be that rarest of bureaucrats, a straight-shooting plain-talker. His give-and-take with reporters is entertaining and even edifying. He does not pull punches and isn't afraid to argue a point with correspondents or call their questions silly or unfounded. He's, ironically perhaps, a joy to watch.

—TOM SHALES, WASHINGTON POST

ONE OF THE MANY TRAITS that have come to define Rumsfeld in his new role as secretary of defense is the appearance of his willingness to say exactly what is on his mind at all times. He is forthright and crotchety and acerbic, all at once, and it was this amalgam that captivated the press corps and the American public in his press briefings in the days after September 11th. Had it not been for those briefings, the Rummy phenomenon would never have come to life.

Before September 11th, most of the relatively few Americans who could name Bush's secretary of defense probably thought of him as an aging, out-of-touch relic of a long-gone administration. But September 11th changed all that, creating an authentic new hero in Washington. *U.S. News & World Report*, in a Rumsfeld cover story compared the secretary of defense to President Harry Truman:

> *He became the Pentagon's answer to Harry Truman,*
> *a straight-talking Midwesterner—via Princeton—who*
> *relished telling the American public that, yes, it is our*
> *mission to kill the enemy in Afghanistan.*

His answers in those now much-anticipated briefings often make the evening news.

When asked if he could define the parameters of the quest for Taliban leaders, Rumsfeld remarked, "I could, but I'm not inclined to." When he doesn't want to answer a probing or potentially revealing question, he'll respond with "I could answer, but I won't, I shan't." On other occasions, he demonstrates a gift for answering directly, even brazenly. For example, when asked about statements issued by the Taliban at a briefing in late 2001, he doesn't mince words. In fact, he practically drips contempt:

> *The reports that we've heard out of the regions have been absolute lying through their teeth, week after week after week, throughout the entire thing.*

One of the most prevalent topics at a Rumsfeld briefing is the possible capture of Osama bin Laden, the man who allegedly planned and organized the terrorist attacks. Rumsfeld brought up the topic when addressing military personnel at Fort Bragg:

> *The question is, how close we are to finding Osama bin Laden. And I honestly have tried to answer that question and I don't know how to answer it well. My feeling is, until you have something, you don't have it.... It's kind of like, as I said, running around the barnyard chasing a chicken; until you get it, you don't have it.*

Most of the time, Rumsfeld seems to be relishing his new role, despite the tragic circumstances that helped to create it. In one briefing in which he and General Tommy R. Franks, commander in chief, Central Command, used a map to highlight certain troop positions, Rumsfeld became gleeful when he was given a laser pointer: "This is fantastic!" proclaimed Rumsfeld. "I've got a laser pointer. Holy mackerel!" When asked by a reporter if his new laser toy was a lethal weapon, Rumsfeld shot back: "It's close! I'll just keep it in my right hand here. It's terrific."

Such an exuberant response could have made the defense secretary seem a bit silly. In this case, the reporters found themselves laughing along with Rumsfeld. This reflects the unusual rapport he had established with the 80 or so reporters who regularly gather for his briefings. As noted, they appreciate his candor and his truth-telling. And they may also figure that if the Pentagon's CEO can lighten up a grave moment, they can, too. It is a delicate balance, but it is important to strike it. In the wake of the worst terrorist attack in American history, humor and self-deprecation—used appropriately—have turned out to be powerful tools.

A NEW BRAND OF PENTAGON CANDOR

Rumsfeld's unique style of communication earned him high marks from the American people. During the first three months of the war on terrorism, Rumsfeld earned an approval rating of close to 80 percent—an astounding level, enjoyed by only a few politicians in recent history. Again, candor, confidence, and command of the situation seemed to be the keys. Americans—so often subjected to euphemisms like "collateral damage" (civilian casualties)—embraced the Rumsfeld style.

Along with the straight talk came a bounty of "Rummyisms." He speaks of "chasing the wrong rabbit," "catching chickens," "feeding an alligator, hoping it eats you last." At the same time, as noted, Rumsfeld isn't afraid to punish the media for "illogical" questions. He once lambasted a reporter for "beginning with an illogical premise and proceeding perfectly logically to an illogical conclusion" (the line that was spoofed on "Saturday Night Live"). At times, Rumsfeld's offbeat style made him sound like an odd, but shrewd, combination of Harry Truman, Ross Perot, and Yogi Berra.

In early 2002, for example, while wrapping up a briefing that dealt with such grave topics as weapons of mass destruction and the death of an army sergeant killed in battle, Rumsfeld said he would take two more questions. That sounded straightforward enough. But the exchange that followed seemed to be lifted straight out of an Abbott and Costello routine and demonstrates Rumsfeld's ability to walk the fine line between humor and gravity:

REPORTER #1: *Mr. Secretary—*

RUMSFELD: *What do you say we have two more questions?*

REPORTER #1: *I was denied a follow-up—*

RUMSFELD: *What do you say we have two more—and you're the first.*

REPORTER #1: *Okay. Thank you. A moment ago, you—*

RUMSFELD: *And you're the second.*

REPORTER #1: *A moment ago—*

REPORTER #2: *That's two.*

REPORTER #1: *I haven't had—*

REPORTER #2: *He hasn't had any.*

REPORTER #1: *A moment ago—*

RUMSFELD: *Neither has, have they?*

REPORTER #2: *He's had two.*

REPORTER #1: *A moment ago you said—*

But war is a solemn game, and Rumsfeld knows it. His acerbic style accomplishes several goals, not the least of which is to keep journalists on their toes. The Rummyisms never compromise the perception of him as a serious leader, and few doubt Rumsfeld's resolve. His colorful asides and witticisms are never misinterpreted as a belittling of the war or an effort to confuse the American electorate. Instead, they are *reassuring*. His audiences take comfort from the fact that he—and we—are able to find shared relief in even the grimmest of circumstances, without lessening our determination.

As noted, Rumsfeld's candor represents a marked departure from the way past wars had been managed. In previous wars, obfuscation ruled the day. In the wake of September 11th, the Rumsfeld communication style indisputably was the right one at the right time. But Rumsfeld's tough talk—and tough actions—haven't always won him friends. In fact, two decades earlier, his no-nonsense, take-no-prisoners approach earned him a not-so-welcome distinction from one of the nation's leading business publications.

ONE OF THE TEN TOUGHEST BOSSES

In 1980, *Fortune* Magazine named Rumsfeld one of the "ten toughest bosses" in America. Rumsfeld, as noted, had taken the top job at pharmaceutical maker G. D. Searle in 1977, and his decisive measures had been effective in turning the company around. But the magazine focused on Rumsfeld's allegedly hard-hearted ways:

> *Sheer intelligence, combined with the will to use it mercilessly, is another characteristic that can make an executive difficult to work for....Rumsfeld's grilling of subordinates can be intense and relentless.*

Fortune described a particularly harsh encounter between Rumsfeld and an unfortunate Searle executive, who was summoned home from a vacation to make a presentation to the chairman. Five minutes into the presentation, Rumsfeld interrupted and began grilling his hapless subordinate. According to this executive, Rumsfeld lacked the patience even to sit through the presentation, and wound up thoroughly unnerving the executive: "It took me a while to get glued back together."

In fairness, the magazine never named the executive, and there is no way of knowing if the offending presentation was what Rumsfeld had asked for in the first place. But the magazine went on to say this about Rumsfeld:

> *His work as a Congressman, Secretary of Defense, and chief of staff in the Ford White House seemed to have honed his ability to sniff out and demolish anyone who is not in complete control of the facts.*

If this is a critique, it is a critique that some cynical executives would be happy to have applied to themselves. Yes, building consensus and establishing trust are important, as Rumsfeld himself has argued. But at the same time, organizations can't flourish if they are led by people who aren't in "control of the facts"—or by people who tolerate fuzziness and imprecision.

RUMSFELD'S WRATH

And it wasn't only those who weren't in command of the facts who suffered through the Rumsfeld fury. Other people, in other circumstances, have told tales of Rumsfeld's alleged excesses.

For example, according to an interview with a former secret service agent from the Nixon-Ford era, who asked not to be identified, Rumsfeld's wrath could be formidable. Once, while escorting a cabinet member through a White House doorway more or less blocked by Rumsfeld and another official, the agent excused himself and touched Rumsfeld lightly above the waist to clear a path and move "his guy" through. An irate Rumsfeld—evidently infuriated that an agent would be so bold as to touch him—dressed him down on the spot. Within minutes, Rumsfeld was on the phone to the head of the Secret Service, demanding that the agent be disciplined (the agent was indeed called by a high-ranking agent who apologetically made his anger known, but the matter was quickly dropped).

Another incident reveals a different side of Rumsfeld's sometimes roughshod ways. According to the *Chicago Tribune*, the Searle chief was displeased when one of his executives gained a lot of weight. Rumsfeld not only made his disapproval known to the manager but also made $10,000 of the overweight executive's annual bonus contingent upon his dropping the offending pounds. The executive—whose name was never revealed—made his weight reduction target and thereby protected his bonus.

Today, such actions by a CEO would almost certainly not be tolerated. A quarter-century ago, though, chief executives could get away with hurling thunderbolts and imposing their personal tastes on their subordinates—and Rumsfeld didn't hesitate to do so. He was in good company, too. For example, four years later, *Fortune* described another leader on their "toughest boss" list, whose style and manner made Rumsfeld sound almost tame by comparison:

> *According to former employees, [this CEO] conducts meetings so aggressively that people tremble. He attacks almost physically with his intellect— criticizing, demeaning, ridiculing, humiliating.... If you have a contradictory idea you have to be willing to take the guff to put it forward.*

An employee's worst nightmare? Perhaps. But this particular boss (who "attacks almost physically") was named "The Ultimate Manager" by the same publication fifteen years later (Jack Welch).

In an interview with *Fortune* for that 1980 cover story, Rumsfeld made no apologies for his style of leadership. Here is how Rumsfeld described the way he would fire an employee who did not "obey" his wishes:

> *You not only let someone who has not been obeying you go, you do it publicly so everyone knows that breaking the rules brings immediate punishment....*
> *We got rid of a bunch for the good of the rest.*

Most exceptional leaders—whether they come from the world of business, professional sports, or the military—have little patience for nonperformers or underachievers. One analyst who followed Rumsfeld's tenure at Searle—Lawrence Smith—described Rumsfeld in 1982 as an "exceptional executive" and emphasized that he was good at both hiring and firing. And it is worth noting that even the "heartless" Rumsfeld—who yelled and fired with little restraint—understood that he needed top-notch people around him to achieve extraordinary things. Here he is in 1984 speaking to *Forbes* reporter John A. Byrne:

> *Unless you're a Mozart, Einstein or Mary Lou Retton, most of what we do in life we do with other people. If you want to do something bigger than any of us, you have to do it with other human beings. I don't know anything more important than that.*

Regardless of how one views Rumsfeld's ultracompetitive, contentious style, there is no doubt that he was an effective, results-driven CEO. If his behavior went "over the top" at times, it was because he could not tolerate failure in any form. And by declining to tolerate failure, he turned Searle (and later General Instrument) into a profitable, growing business, and made himself rich in the process.

Later, in his second tour of duty at the Pentagon, he would once again demonstrate his complex leadership style: highly competent, extraordinarily demanding. And this time, there would be far more riding on the outcome.

LET COMMUNICATION FIT THE SITUATION

Perhaps the key lesson from these examples of Rumsfeld's communication methods has to do with the importance of situational leadership—employing the right communication style at the right time. Clearly, Rumsfeld's Pentagon briefings have captivated a nation of skeptics who are more accustomed to hearing a prevarication than a provocative retort. The following exchange on NBC's "Meet the Press" makes the point:

> TIM RUSSERT: *Do you think we have a few months of long, bloody battle?*
>
> RUMSFELD: *"Oh, I wouldn't limit it to that."*

That response is honest, direct, and classic Rumsfeld. In the past, politicians would do anything to convince Americans that wars would be short and body counts would be low. Rumsfeld—eager to underpromise and overdeliver—has taken the opposite approach in his handling of the media coverage of the war.

To some extent, the approach is a calculated one. Rumsfeld is not unaware of the impact his "outspoken" ways can have. Here's how he put it in an interview with the *Washington Post* in late 2001:

*I am very blunt; I'm very outspoken...and
it is entirely possible that I may have
said something at one point or another that
could lead some observer to want to characterize
it that way, but sometimes I do those things
simply to stimulate thought and challenge
people, to press them, probe them, see if
they've thought something through....*

THE RUMSFELD WAY

Be yourself: Above all, Rumsfeld has been himself from the very beginning. His soaring popularity was not about his reinventing himself but instead about his style's being the right one at the right time.

Speak your mind, even if it means making people uncomfortable: The Rumsfeld phenomenon grows directly out of this individual's willingness to say exactly what is on his mind. Consider exhibiting that level of candor in your own workplace: What would happen?

Don't be afraid to say, "I don't know": Rumsfeld won accolades for admitting when he didn't know something. He has bluntly criticized politicians for never wanting to admit that they didn't know something.

Use humor even in tough times: Rumsfeld has shown that there is a place for humor even in the gravest of situations—and this lesson comes from a man not known for his jovial ways. Incorporate humor in your everyday communication, particularly when colleagues in the workplace appear to need it most.

Underpromise and overdeliver: Rumsfeld has been careful not to declare victory in Afghanistan until all the campaign's ambitious objectives are met, including the elimination of the Taliban, Osama bin Laden, and the al Qaeda terrorist network.

ALL THE RIGHT MOVES

Position Yourself for Success

*Fortune often favors those that have the rare gift
of being in the right place at the right time. Even
rarer, however, is the knack of being somewhere
else. Donald Rumsfeld possessed both.*

—ROBERT T. HARTMANN, CHIEF OF STAFF

FOR VICE PRESIDENT FORD

*I don't consider being ruthless incompatible
with being a great statesman.*

—HENRY KISSINGER, FEBRUARY 2002

MAKING THE RIGHT MOVE at the right time has been a hallmark of Rumsfeld's career. Many a politician and political pundit have written about Rumsfeld's uncanny ability to disappear at exactly the correct time and then return when a particular tide had turned.

To some, it might have seemed that good things just *happened* to Rumsfeld—maybe they were just the results of an enviable string of luck. But according to Robert T. Hartmann, Ford's chief of staff as vice president (and longtime *Los Angeles Times* correspondent), Rumsfeld was aided by an instinct honed during his years as a wrestling champion:

> *Everything in Rummy's life seemed to come early and easily. But this was deceptive. He was a cool and careful planner. As a politician, he recognized and respected fate; as a wrestler, he was even more alert for an opening to take fate by the forelock.*

In his 1999 memoir, Henry Kissinger—who had his share of run-ins with Rumsfeld during the Ford years—called him the most "formidable new arrival in the Ford White House." Kissinger praised Rumsfeld for his political savvy and for his recognition of the dramatic changes in the national mood in 1974: "As a veteran of the political wars,

Rumsfeld understood better than I that Watergate and Vietnam were likely to evoke a conservative backlash...."

The truth was, however, that Kissinger and other Ford staffers were suspicious of Rumsfeld from the start. Many saw him as a hard-hearted politician who would do anything to advance his own fortunes. Ford insider Hartmann once asked Rumsfeld straight out about his ambitions:

*I once asked him, half in fun, if his ambition was
to be president of the United States. Half in fun,
he answered that his ambition had been
trained one step at a time, to do each job well
without neglecting to watch for the next, better one.
It seemed a good formula....*

That was part of the Rumsfeld method, of course. Like any calculating strategist, he was always planning his next move. This has been a Rumsfeld constant throughout his careeer: for example, five days after the terrorist attacks, in planning sessions with the president and his team, Rumsfeld remarked: "This is chess, not checkers. We must be thinking beyond the first move." So even before the U.S. had implemented step one, Rumsfeld was anticipating the next three or four moves down the line.

At the same time, however, he has always maintained a laser-like focus on the task at hand. This twofold approach manifested itself early in Rumsfeld's political career—in fact, dating back to his opening moves in the political arena—and perhaps explains why seemingly long odds did not discourage him from throwing his hat into the ring.

DEFY SKEPTICS

At the age of twenty-nine, following a few years of working for an Ohio representative and at an investment banking firm, Rumsfeld entered and subsequently won a congressional primary and then went on to defeat his Democratic opponent handily. Had he not had the confidence to enter the political waters so early, the Rumsfeld story might never have been written. Two decades later, Rumsfeld attributed his success to his willingness to defy skeptics and risk defeat:

> *There are always risks, but I am used to risks. I ran for Congress....when I was twenty-nine years old and there weren't many people around who thought I had much of a chance to win. It seems like an incredible decision now. But it proved right.*

The four terms that Rumsfeld served in Congress positioned him for the Nixon and Ford appointments. But it is important to note that in Rumsfeld's career (as in most people's careers), things did not simply fall into place. Each move was a measured one, and—as mentioned earlier—earned him enemies along the way.

Successful leaders often present paradoxes, and Rumsfeld is no exception. While few have questioned Rumsfeld's integrity, he nevertheless became known as a self-interested politician whose moves were most politely described as "cunning." The *Washington Post* summed up Rumsfeld's career in late 2001:

> *After three terms he joined the Nixon administration and in succeeding years became known as a maestro of the stealthy bureaucratic maneuver, the calculated leak, the hidden power play.*

Others have used harsher words to describe both Rumsfeld and his tactics. But those who have examined his record carefully would most likely agree on one point, at least: that he helped create his own luck, each step along the way. In fact, one of his earliest and wisest moves removed him from one of the gravest situations in political history.

SIDESTEPPING WATERGATE

By 1972, Rumsfeld had completed his stint as head of the OEO and was serving as director of the CLC. When he accepted the position as ambassador to NATO in 1972, Rumsfeld removed himself from several situations that could have stalled his career, if not ended it. As noted earlier, he had no involvement in Watergate; but had he opted to stay in the U.S., he might have been tainted by proximity to illegal acts.

We should remember, too, that the economy was also in bad shape, as prices and inflation soared. Instead of putting himself in the line of fire—where he surely would have been had he stayed at the CLC—he spent eighteen months as ambassador to NATO, living in Brussels with his family while gaining valuable military and diplomatic experience. Good moves by any measure—but it was his next moves that would accelerate his career, and at the same time inflame the wrath of many fellow Republicans.

When Nixon resigned and Ford called in Rumsfeld, the NATO ambassador came to Washington, where he spent several weeks heading an interim task force to organize the transition. Rumsfeld said he had no interest in a permanent Ford cabinet post, and both Ford and Rumsfeld agreed that this would be only an interim position that would last no longer than a month. Rumsfeld made his recommendations and then flew back to Brussels to resume his NATO duties.

When Ford pardoned Nixon in early September, thinking he was doing the nation a service by ending the torments of Watergate, the results were disastrous. Except for diehard Nixon loyalists, most Americans felt that Nixon deserved no special treatment, and deserved to stand trial for any misdeeds. (Indeed, some raised the specter that Nixon and Ford had struck an unholy bargain: a resignation for a pardon.) Once again, Rumsfeld was thousands of miles away, thereby avoiding the stink most Americans associated with the Nixon pardon.

"RUMSFELD'S MACHINATIONS"

After the disaster of the pardon, Ford reassessed his staff. This reassessment ultimately meant that NATO lost Rumsfeld as an ambassador, as Ford convinced Rumsfeld to take the job of chief of staff (although Rumsfeld preferred the term "staff coordinator"). To Rumsfeld, the job had the dual advantages of helping the new president and moving his own career a giant step forward. But how Ford got Rumsfeld to "agree to take the job" and how Rumsfeld essentially dictated the terms of the offer reveal a great deal about the Rumsfeld way.

Although he stood to gain enormous power, Rumsfeld once again told Ford that he didn't want the job: "I'm not the guy to do it, and I don't have any desire to do it," he declared. "You'd be much better off with someone else." (Rumsfeld had a history of playing hard to get when it came to new positions.) But Ford would not relent. He needed a strong hand, and he needed one fast. Things were getting worse by the week.

One of the reasons why Rumsfeld played hard to get, Ford later recalled, was that he felt that the job simply could not be done, at least not in the way Ford had structured the position. Rumsfeld knew that Ford was running the White House with a "spokes-of-the-wheel" model, which gave every member of the Cabinet equal access to the president. Rumsfeld knew this organizational model was deeply flawed. A "spokes of the wheel model" is known as a "collegial model" of decision making, one in which a group of co-equal subordinates compete for authority. The problem was that this model is simply the wrong one for a White House environment. If a dozen aides were permitted equal access to the Oval Office, the president would have a difficult time getting anything done. In reality, it is usually a group of four to seven aides who have this privilege in a hierarchical model. These are usually the chief of staff, deputy chief of staff, NSC Director, sometimes the press secretary, and an additional one or two aides of the president's choosing.

Rumsfeld therefore told Ford that the only way he would take the post was on *his* terms. He began by telling Ford his opinion of the "spokes-of-the-wheel" model:

> *It won't work. You don't have the time to*
> *run the administrative machinery at the*
> *White House yourself. I know you don't want a*
> *Haldeman-type chief of staff, but someone has*
> *to fill that role, and unless I have that authority,*
> *I won't be able to serve you effectively.*

In his memoir, Ford remarked that Rumsfeld "was right. Everyone wanted a portion of my time, my accessibility was making me fair game for ridiculous requests and the spokes of the wheel structure wasn't working well. Without a strong decision-maker who could help me set my priorities, I'd be hounded to death by gnats and flies....I told Rummy that I recognized this and that with his help, I could begin to do something about it."

Historians and Ford insiders alike have suggested that Rumsfeld wasn't above the political fray—that despite the fact that he was fiercely loyal to the president, he nevertheless brought his own agenda to the Ford White House. This begins to explain some of the hostility between Rumsfeld and other high-level staffers. Robert Hartmann also attributed a large part of the problem to the fact that Rumsfeld was a "Nixon holdover." According to Hartmann, Ford's biggest mistake was that he opted for a continuation of Nixon's White House, leaving many of the Nixon appointees in place. They became "Ford's Praetorian Guard," Hartmann wrote—a "fifth column dedicated to Ford's failure."

While Ford remained convinced that he had done the right thing in bringing in Rumsfeld, many felt that Rumsfeld manipulated the course of events over the ensuing eighteen months. Some Ford insiders dubbed Rumsfeld a "smiling Haldeman." Some have claimed that Rumsfeld engineered Haig's departure as chief of staff and, later, Vice President Rockefeller's removal from the 1976 ticket. Again, to be fair, Haig says nothing of Rumsfeld's alleged scheming in his own candid and detailed memoir, so there is ample room for doubt.

John Osborne, who covered Ford for *The New Republic* (and who was also the key White House reporter of the day) put it this way: Ford was "being served by the weakest staff in recent White House history." And as a result, "Ford's own ineptitude had created the opening for Rumsfeld's machinations." Regardless of Rumsfeld's motives (which even Kissinger called "honorable"), two facts seem irrefutable: Rumsfeld dictated the terms under which he would assume one of most powerful positions in government—White House chief of staff—and he skillfully exercised the power that he had assigned to himself.

GAIN TRUST TO GAIN POWER

Where did this power lie? In several areas. First, as "staff coordinator"—the name that Rumsfeld insisted on using instead of "chief of staff"—"Rummy" was able to install many of his own allies within the White House and throughout the administration. Second, he was the gatekeeper to the president, spending more time with him than any other member of the staff, including Henry Kissinger. Rumsfeld's purposeful reorganization of the White House lessened the influence of every other member of the staff while bolstering his own position (see Chapter 6 for more on this subject).

Few things went on inside the White House without Rumsfeld's awareness and concurrence. He had "the most intimate knowledge of who saw Ford, for how long, and the problems discussed," according to Pulitzer Prize-winning journalist Clark Mollenhoff, Washington bureau chief for the *Des Moines Register*:

> *He could set the stage, pamper the star, Jerry Ford,
> and essentially be the director, producer and writer
> for any scenario Ford wanted to present to the nation
> or to secure his political future. As long as the leading
> man's part was augmented, or protected, Don
> Rumsfeld could write his own ending.*

Mollenhoff went on to say that Rumsfeld had more power than Haldeman under Nixon and was setting the stage for his next move: into a major cabinet position. In Mollenhoff's opinion, even before Rumsfeld assumed a top cabinet post, he had become one of the two most powerful men in the United States:

> *Within ten and a half months after Rumsfeld
> announced the reorganization to put Ford's*

house in order, the young man from Illinois had
solidified his hold on the White House and was
recognized as the most powerful man in Washington,
second only to the president himself.

How did Rumsfeld—who had claimed he didn't want the job in the first place—pull off what many regarded as a power grab? Or, phrased more charitably, how was he able to dominate the Ford agenda so thoroughly? The answer is as relatively uncomplicated as Gerald Ford himself. Ford trusted Rumsfeld. In the House, he had been one of Ford's most capable and loyal lieutenants and had helped Ford immensely (at some cost to himself) during Ford's rise to a position of authority in the House. At the same time, he was no toady, no bootlicker, and wise leaders value the people around them who are brave enough to say "no" to the boss. As Ford later wrote:

Above all, he was a superior administrator, and a
demon when it came to working long hours,
organizing an office, and making sure that everything
functioned efficiently....Don had no qualms about
telling me when I was wrong.

So Rumsfeld came into the White House with Ford's confidence, and everything he did in the White House was designed to reinforce and build that confidence. Rumsfeld certainly traded on his deep understanding of Ford, but he also afforded the President a measure of respect that others did not. As Hartmann later put it:

Rumsfeld had an enormous advantage over Haig and
the other Praetorians....Rummy was also a student of
Gerald R. Ford. The rest held the new president in

*almost open contempt. They considered him and his
cronies as sorely in need of their sophisticated
knowledge of presidential behavior. Rumsfeld knew
better. He knew he would have to carry out 90 percent
of what Ford wanted in order to get 10 percent of
what he wanted. And he was too smart to take on
other longtime Ford favorites in a frontal showdown.*

This passage reveals much about Rumsfeld's strategic
nature. At each point in his career, he seemed to have the
next success formula in his head. In addition, his take-no-
prisoners style of leadership, combined with his absolute
control over staffing, meant that he didn't put up with
troublemakers. Throughout his reign at the Ford White
House, he demonstrated his impatience for people who did
not subscribe to his view of the world. He took this atti-
tude with him into the private sector, and this is one reason
why he emerged as such a forceful and effective CEO a few
years later. In late 2001, Rumsfeld reflected on his hard-
charging personal style to the *Washington Post*:

*I work long hours and seven days a week, and I'll ask
somebody to do something and I will be absolutely
certain I asked them two and half weeks ago and it
will turn out it was two and half or three days ago.
I have a certain amount of impatience about things.
I like to get things done.*

He likes to get things *done.* He also likes those around
him to get things done—preferably his way, and on his
schedule.

THE RUMSFELD WAY

"Take fate by the forelock": Look for the openings (or, as coach Vince Lombardi once put it, "run to daylight"). Much of Rumsfeld's success was due to making sure that he was in the right place at the right time. He never missed an opportunity to advance his own agenda (even if it meant that another cabinet member would lose influence).

Avoid any appearance of impropriety: One of the keys to Rumsfeld's being out of the Watergate line of fire was that he knew not to get involved with the top Nixon aides (e.g. Haldeman), whom he did not trust. That steered him into the NATO post, which kept him out of harm's way twice: first during Watergate and then during the Nixon pardon.

Manage your career like a chess game: Keep your mind on the "next step." Rumsfeld "had been trained one step at a time, to do each job well without neglecting to watch for the next, better one." His careful planning paid big dividends, putting him in the right place at the right time throughout a four-decade-long career.

Don't be afraid to tell the boss when you think he or she is wrong: One of the reasons Rumsfeld gained so much power was that Ford trusted him. He did so because his chief of staff was not afraid to tell him the truth, even if he knew it wasn't what Ford wanted to hear.

CRAFTING COALITIONS

Dealing with Friends and Foes

Mr. Rumsfeld...also seems to be the prime shaper
of the modern, flexible sort of alliance that
America is trying to assemble.

—THE ECONOMIST

This war will not be waged by a grand alliance united for a single purpose of defeating an axis of hostile powers. Instead, it will involve floating coalitions of countries, which may change and evolve. Countries will have different roles and contribute in different ways.

—DONALD H. RUMSFELD, SEPTEMBER 2001

RUMSFELD'S IMPRESSIVE RESUME, which included a NATO ambassadorship as well as a stint as secretary of defense, prepared him well for his second tour of duty as head of the Pentagon. Rumsfeld learned early on how to amass and wield power, as well as how to navigate the muddy waters of international diplomacy.

Throughout his career, he has demonstrated an uncanny knack for making the right friends, avoiding the wrong enemies, and engineering events so that he ends up on the winning side. He has demonstrated the streetfighter's ability to amass personal power, but he has also shown that he can operate as a statesman, such as when he helped put together the international coalition to conduct a war against terrorism.

Examining his record provides some valuable insights into Rumsfeld the tactician and how he deftly manages to consolidate power under very different sets of circumstances. In this chapter, in order to shed insight on the range of Rumsfeld's abilities, we will move chronologically through three separate situations that spanned more than three decades.

BACKING THE RIGHT HORSE

The morning after the 1964 presidential election was a truly bleak juncture for the Republican party. Lyndon Johnson had trounced Barry Goldwater, and lots of Republicans had gone down with the conservative Arizona senator. In the new Eighty-ninth Congress, the Republican numbers would be reduced to 140, the worst showing since Alf Landon was defeated by Franklin Roosevelt in 1936.

The young and ambitious Congressman Rumsfeld was anything but despondent, however. In fact, he was hell-bent on shaking things up and bringing change to a stodgy party. He became a leading figure in a group of Republicans whom Gerald Ford dubbed the "Young Turks"—although others referred to them as "Rumsfeld's Raiders." The Raiders felt that the GOP was in dire need of change, starting with its leadership. They were determined to reinvigorate their party, infusing it with new blood and a new (more moderate) mission. One of the major obstacles they faced, however, was the entrenched minority leader, conservative Republican Charlie Halleck.

The Raiders came together out of frustration with the status quo, determined to seize the levers of power. Here is how Wil Hylton described the coup in *Esquire*:

> *One Thursday in 1964...the future opened up. It started with a ringing phone. Everybody calling at once....They'd decided to stage a coup in the House, and they wanted his [Rumsfeld's] help. He headed back to Washington that night, got in at 2:00 A.M., and was holding meetings by 9:00 the next morning.*

On that day, the Raiders vowed to change the DNA of the party by moving it more to the center. They felt that Goldwater had taken the party in the wrong direction—

much too far to the right. Only by getting in their own candidate as minority leader would they have the chance to get control of the party. The Turks knew they were on dangerous ground as they set out to oust Halleck, since the elder Republican had many powerful friends in Congress. If the coup failed, retribution would be swift and sure. Hylton described the pact that Rumsfeld's group made that day, which amounted to a major shift in the party:

> *It wasn't personal....It was about youth and power and the bare-naked fact that they wanted to guide the Republican party to the mainstream and to dominance. It was about, as Rummy said in a 1964 interview that was never published, the fact that 'Jerry' [Representative Gerald Ford] was considered to be a reasonable vehicle."*

Because the post would give Gerald Ford a better chance of becoming Speaker of the House—Ford's lifelong ambition—he agreed to challenge Halleck. The Turks knew Halleck had many friends on the Hill, which meant that the race was likely to be close. Ultimately, a young Kansas representative named Robert Dole may have made the difference, since it was he who convinced a five-member Kansas delegation to throw its votes to Ford. When all votes were counted, Ford defeated Halleck by a mere six votes (73–67).

Why is this ancient political history relevant to today's story? Because it illustrates some of Rumsfeld's enduring leadership traits. While he has often exhibited maverick-like tendencies, he has also believed that putting the right people in the right place, and backing them up, can make the difference between success and failure. Oftentimes this involves taking calculated risks. Among Rumsfeld's Rules is an aphorism that he has quoted from former Harvard president James B. Conant:

> *Behold the turtle. He makes progress*
> *only when he sticks his neck out.*

Through forty years of service in both the public and private sectors, Rumsfeld has stuck his neck out many times—although never without carefully calculating his odds ahead of time. And if making progress equates to making enemies along the way, then so be it.

RUMSFELD'S REORGANIZATION: FIRST AMONG EQUALS

For our second example, let's fast-forward to an event a decade later. In the fall of 1974, following the Nixon resignation and the Ford transition, Rumsfeld was back in the West Wing of the White House, setting up shop in the old "corner pocket" suite of offices once occupied by Nixon aides Haldeman and Haig. By now, Rumsfeld had a relationship with the new president that dated back more than a decade. In his new role as Ford's "staff coordinator," he would reorganize the jumbled Nixon-Ford staff. He intended to waste little time in getting started.

Ford didn't always advance the cause. Privately, Ford had agreed that Rumsfeld should be in charge of regulating access to the Oval Office. At the meeting in which Ford formally introduced Rumsfeld to the White House staff, he made more or less that same point again. But then he added, apparently as an afterthought, that his "door would always remain open." Rumsfeld noted the contradiction, but held his tongue. He already knew how he would resolve that problem.

On December 19th, the Rumsfeld plan for reorganizing the White House staff was unveiled. Rumsfeld proclaimed that the reorganization was intended "to put the house in order." Rumsfeld pointedly said that this was now "*President Ford's* White House" and that "his approach and working style [are] reflected in this organization."

At first blush, the reorganization charts that had been approved by President Ford did not appear to give Rumsfeld more power than other members of the cabinet. The truth was that the new plan consolidated Rumsfeld's power base while reducing the power of other White House insiders. According to Robert Hartmann, Rumsfeld "deftly sold" to Ford the ideas that the new plan would help to create an "open" administration and that—if it were implemented— "the Haldeman-Haig iron curtain was a relic of the past."

Here's how Hartmann described the exchange that took place when Rumsfeld explained the new organization:

> Q: *Can you tell us whose authority has been enhanced and whose authority has been diminished?*
>
> Rumsfeld: *Yes, the President's authority is enhanced.*
>
> Q: *Mr. Rumsfeld, I see your name in more boxes than anyone else's. Does this mean that you are the chief aide, the first among equals?*
>
> Rumsfeld: *No....He wanted me to be in charge of the administrative part, and he also wanted me to serve in a coordinating responsibility—and he does a lot of the coordinating himself.*

The plan, according to the *Des Moines Register*'s Clark Mollenhoff, did indeed put more power in Rumsfeld's hands than in anyone else's, despite the fact that there were three others who, at least on paper, had equal access to

Ford. Mollenhoff declared Rumsfeld the "victor" in the new administration:

If not the hero, he was definitely the victor; a victor who had manipulated the organization to flow, if not through him, at least within his reach. He could maneuver hand- picked aides into key positions in the White House and in agencies.

One of the hand-picked aides that Rumsfeld installed was another Rumsfeld loyalist: his young deputy, Dick Cheney. Cheney had proven himself as Rumsfeld's assistant in the White House and as his "alter ego" at OEO. His official title became "Deputy Assistant to the President." Clearly, in Hartmann's view at least, Rumsfeld took great care to populate the landscape with individuals who owed a debt to, and would look out for, Donald Rumsfeld.

In fairness, it should be mentioned that Hartmann—who had served Ford since 1966 as a top aide—almost certainly had an ax to grind with Rumsfeld. Once Ford became President, Hartmann lost direct access to Ford, and he became increasingly unhappy with many of the changes that were made—particularly when Rumsfeld moved Hartmann's office out of the West Wing to a more remote location.

Rumsfeld had engineered Hartmann's exile by explaining that the President needed that office as a place to relax. Hartmann, long-time Ford ally, speechwriter and confidant, was mortified. Rumsfeld further irked Hartmann by editing his speeches and passing them out to the staff for comment. It was these tactics that confirmed Rumsfeld's coup, a seizing of power that was completed within a few months of his arrival in the Ford White House.

In early 2002, Esquire's Wil Hylton put his own spin on what Rumsfeld had achieved in the Ford White House:

"There was almost no higher for Rumsfeld to go...Every morning, he was the first to see the president of the United States and he was the last to see him at night. He was one of the most prominent and promising members of his party....It was time, at last, to plateau."

GAIN POWER BY GIVING SOME AWAY

For our third example, let's look a little more closely at Rumsfeld's most significant experience in the private sector. After Ford's loss to Jimmy Carter in the 1976 election, Rumsfeld decided he wanted more balance in his life. He dabbled briefly in academia, but he had bigger things in mind. In 1977, as noted in previous chapters, he accepted the position of CEO of pharmaceutical company G. D. Searle. That experience is illuminating, because it shows us how Rumsfeld wields power on a stage far away from the political arena.

First, a bit of Searle history: Gideon Daniel Searle started a drugstore business in 1888 and founded the company that bore his name in 1908 in Chicago. After creating a substantial Midwestern market for certain elixirs and salves that were sold directly to doctors, Searle died in 1917. The company was passed on from generation to generation, and in 1966, when the grandson of the founder stepped down, a "troika" of three managers was appointed to run the business. Two of the three were Searles—Dan and Bill Searle—and the third, Wes Dixon, had married into the family.

By 1977, the troika realized that things weren't working. None of the three saw themselves as suited for the role of CEO, and the triumvirate had great difficulty making operating decisions, let alone reaching consensus on corporate objectives. They therefore decided to bring in a new leader from the outside. The three made a list of criteria and candidates, and one name kept rising to the top: Donald Rumsfeld. They had followed Rumsfeld's career ever since he ran successfully for Congress at the age of twenty-nine. Although he was far from a seasoned executive—in fact, he had almost no private sector experience—he was a proven organizer and motivator of people, and he was a prodigiously hard worker. They offered Rumsfeld the job, and he accepted, taking up his duties in June 1977.

Rumsfeld knew that this particular job came with an abundance of baggage. First, and most important, the troika was not going away. This meant they would have to be consulted on key decisions. Based on Rumsfeld's history, one might have expected him to demand complete authority. But perhaps sensing the limits on how far he could push the three family members, Rumsfeld ducked the issue—wisely, as it turned out, because Dan Searle later confessed that he and his two colleagues would never have acceded to such a demand from Rumsfeld.

The upshot was that Rumsfeld would have to run the company and appease the troika at the same time. This was probably even more difficult than it sounds. The company was in relatively dire straits, meaning that Rumsfeld would have to make massive changes to make it competitive again. This would almost certainly prompt individuals and groups to try to go around him and appeal to the longtime owners and leaders of the company. So despite Rumsfeld's tendency to want to move quickly and do things *his* way, he knew that he would have to move carefully and make allies:

> *It was just a recognition that one person has only one head, two arms, and two legs. No one at the top can know everything, so you delegate massive chunks, you create multiple leadership centers.*

One of Rumsfeld's first compromises with the three managers concerned the location of their offices. (In both the public and private sectors, Rumsfeld evidently knew, it was important to allocate offices in ways that reinforced the lines of authority: physical proximity to power matters.) The three agreed to move out of the Searle headquarters building and across the plaza into a separate office tower. That gave Rumsfeld some much-needed breathing room. Nevertheless, according to Joseph McCann, author of a book on Searle and the creation of NutraSweet (*Sweet Success*, 1990), Rumsfeld still had to do business in a "fishbowl." In his early years at Searle, he had to demonstrate his "willingness to consult broadly across the firm, and to keep Dan, Bill and Wes involved in the decision-making progress."

At Searle—unlike his strategy at the Ford White House—Rumsfeld consolidated his power inch by inch, through a hundred small victories. Dan Searle, for example, became a Rumsfeld believer when—on an overseas plane ride to Japan—he saw Rumsfeld reading a thick book on Japanese emperors in order to gain a better understanding of the Japanese culture. Gradually, the troika became convinced that they had selected the right man for the job—and, gradually, Rumsfeld gathered up the reins of authority.

BUILDING A WARTIME COALITION

On the morning following the September 11th attacks, a wide variety of possible responses were being weighed in the cramped spaces of the White House War Room. One such response would be to wage an international war on terrorism, seeking out and destroying terrorist networks and bases wherever they existed in the world. But this would be one of the most difficult paths, because it would require the rapid assembly of an international coalition of nations—each of which would have to be cultivated and participate according to terms that were acceptable both to themselves and to the United States.

It was a perilous path, but it appeared to be the right one. So, in an inspired speech reminiscent of Roosevelt's "Day of Infamy" address in the wake of Pearl Harbor, President Bush addressed a joint session of Congress in the week following the attacks as follows:

> *This is not...just America's fight....This is the world's fight. This is civilization's fight. This is the fight of all who believe in progress and pluralism, tolerance and freedom. We ask every nation to join us. We will ask, and we will need, the help of police forces, intelligence services, and banking systems around the world....An attack on one is an attack on all.*

The responsibility of building the necessary coalition fell largely on the shoulders of Colin Powell. However, Donald Rumsfeld also had a role to play, although much of it went on behind the scenes (see Chapter 8 for more on Rumsfeld's part in building the coalition). The most critical piece of the puzzle, U.S. officials knew, was Pakistan. It shared a 1,500-mile border with Afghanistan, would be an indispensable staging ground for certain kinds of operations, and—assuming things went very well—would be the terrorists' most likely destination when escaping from Afghanistan.

So the stakes were enormous. When *Time* magazine asked Bush how he knew that Pakistani President Pervez Musharraf would take the American side, the President answered impassively: "Because I trust Colin Powell and Don Rumsfeld."

This Bush statement of support was significant for many reasons. Powell, who was the administration's most capable coalition builder, had been derided by the press days earlier for being marginalized and out of step with the new administration. In a September 10th cover story, *Time* Magazine had asked, "Where have you gone Colin Powell?" Donald Rumsfeld had his own problems. Earlier in the year he had been perceived as arrogant and high-handed at a NATO defense meeting in which he outlined the U.S. plan to build "Star Wars" defenses. However, in the crucial days and weeks following September 11th, the landscape had shifted dramatically, but Bush never lost faith in these two key cabinet members.

Bush's confidence was not misplaced. Musharraf did indeed become a U.S. ally. And from the first days of the conflict, Rumsfeld emerged as an engaged and thoroughly prepared secretary of defense who understood the mission and the multifaceted role of the coalition:

Another key turning point was the decision
that we would not have a single coalition, but rather
we would use floating coalitions or multiple
coalitions and recognize that because this would be
long, because it would be difficult, and because
different countries have different circumstances,
different perspectives, and different problems,
that we needed their help on a basis that they
were comfortable giving it to us and we would
not...expect everyone to do everything.

So crafting an effective coalition—one that was flexible and reflected the shifting realities of the many nations who might be willing to involve themselves in it—was of critical importance. Working together, the Bush administration pulled off the unlikely—not only enlisting linchpin Pakistan but also gaining back-channel support from a number of nations that were traditional foes of the United States in the international arena.

Back the right horse: It was Rumsfeld's backing of Ford in 1965 as minority leader that put him on the path to selection as chief of staff following Nixon's resignation. Rumsfeld was primarily motivated by a sincere desire to recast his party—but as later events amply demonstrated, he also picked the right horse.

Don't be afraid to "stick your neck out": Throughout his career, Rumsfeld took dozens of calculated risks: running for Congress at age twenty-nine, backing dark horses like Ford, signing up with a troubled White House, moving into the private sector, and so on. Each move caused problems, but the problems were far outweighed by the advantages they created for Rumsfeld.

To consolidate power in an organization, put the right people in the right places: Although Rumsfeld made enemies within the Ford White House as a result of his "methods," he insisted on putting people in whom he had confidence in key positions. The network he created greatly increased his influence and effectiveness—his new enemies notwithstanding.

Don't always insist on complete control: Sometimes the best way to gain power is to demonstrate that you are willing to share it. Had Rumsfeld insisted on running Searle entirely on his own from the outset, for example, he would not have been offered the job in the first place.

Identify key allies early on and know what they can do for you: One of the keys to building a broad-based coalition in the fight against terrorism was figuring out exactly which countries were needed and exactly what each would be able to contribute. Some countries had to take a visible role; others could maintain a low profile. This lesson seems increasingly important in the private sector, where the development of strategic alliances is a more and more important part of the success formula.

7

THE CONSEQUENCE OF VALUES

Moral Leadership and the Responsibility of Office

Let every nation know, whether it wishes us well or ill, that we shall pay any price, bear any burden, meet any hardship, support any friend, oppose any foe to assure the survival and success of liberty. This much we pledge—and more.

—JOHN F. KENNEDY, INAUGURAL ADDRESS, JANUARY 20, 1961

We need to strengthen our ties to democratic allies and to challenge regimes hostile to our interests and values. We need to accept responsibility for America's unique role in preserving and extending an international order friendly to our security, our prosperity and our principles.

—THE PROJECT FOR A NEW AMERICAN CENTURY,

SIGNED BY DONALD RUMSFELD AND OTHERS

ONE OF THE KEYS to effective leadership—in any situation—is an adherence to a core set of values that are not abandoned, qualified, or diluted, even in the most dire circumstances. Without this kind of steadfastness, even a "successful" leader will lose the trust of key constituencies, and this will eventually hamper his or her ability to lead.

In describing the presidency, Franklin Delano Roosevelt spoke of the importance of "moral leadership." Harry Truman wrote, "It is the business of the president to meet situations as they arise, and to meet them in the public interest." Of course, Donald Rumsfeld is not the president (and by this point, he presumably has given up whatever aspirations he may have had about occupying that office). But especially in wartime, the secretary of defense has an enormous opportunity—and responsibility—to exercise moral leadership.

From the first moments of the tragedy, it became increasingly clear that Rumsfeld would play an enormous role in the war on terrorism. According to the *Washington Post*, Bush had phoned Rumsfeld on September 11th from a secure phone on Air Force One, informing him that he had already decided on military action and that it would be he, Rumsfeld, who would execute it: "We'll clean up the mess, and then the ball will be in your court," Bush declared to Rumsfeld that fateful afternoon.

This was not surprising since President Bush is known to be a leader who delegates to an extraordinary extent. The point was underscored in a recent *Time* article, which quoted an unnamed senior military official on interactions with Bush: "When military decisions were brought to him, he'd say, 'Don't bring this to me. I've given you a task, and I have full confidence in you to carry it out.'"

So Rumsfeld is squarely in the "moral spotlight" as he carries out an extremely difficult task delegated to him by Bush. What do we know about his moral compass? As noted in earlier chapters, Rumsfeld has had no qualms about rolling over people who stand between him and his goals. Some of his tactics have been questionable, at best—especially when seen through the lens of early twenty-first-century business practices. But despite recurrent controversy, Rumsfeld has embodied a consistent set of values throughout his career. And although his moral guideline may be criticized for being simplistic, or even negative—"Don't do anything that you would not like to see on the front page of the *Washington Post*"—it appears to have served him well over the years.

"VALUES HAVE CONSEQUENCES"

In 1985, while Rumsfeld was still serving as CEO in the private sector, he was invited to speak at the Ethics and Public Policy Center in Washington, D.C. In his speech, entitled "Values Have Consequences," Rumsfeld reflected on America's global role and on the importance of the role of values in preserving our freedoms. At one point, he issued an interesting challenge to his audience—and, by extension, to his fellow Americans. In doing so, he draws on a quote from Adlai Stevenson:

*A challenge to strive to put into practice the principle
that 'values have consequences,' so that this
'magnificent gamble' that is America can fulfill its
promise and enable more to know the 'inner air in
which freedom lives, and which a man can draw a
breath of self respect.'*

Rumsfeld also spoke at length on the importance of freedom and values and on "how only a clear understanding of and staunch adherence to free values can sustain freedom." In other words, abandoning the moral high ground (at least as Rumsfeld defined it) would be a prescription for a larger defeat:

*The day we lose sight of the distinction between
freedom and the denial of freedom, that is the day
that our global competition ceases to have a moral
dimension and reverts to a struggle that free people
are ill-suited to win.*

Throughout the speech, there is a theme of free will and voluntarism—an emphasis on the fact that being "American" is more a state of mind than an inherited state or an accident of circumstance. And this imposes a moral burden on those who would be "Americans."

*Most Americans...became Americans because of an
idea—a conscious decision made by them or their
ancestors to build a new life in a new land....and the
new life they hoped to build in a setting of freedom,
tolerance, and opportunity.*

Obviously, when one accepts an invitation to speak at an Ethics and Public Policy Center, one assumes a responsibil-

ity to think lofty thoughts and deliver an uplifting challenge to one's audience. But read in its entirety, Rumsfeld's
speech sounds like an authentic statement from someone
who has thought carefully about moral responsibility. He
speaks of "respect for individual rights...individual responsibilities, a government chosen by and accountable to the
people, and equality of opportunity." He decreed that
"these [qualities] form the ethical basis of the American
system."

Rumsfeld's other writings, chiefly his Rules aphorisms,
take these grandiose ideas to a more practical level and
provide additional insight into Rumsfeld's value system.
Here he speaks of integrity, of "serving the public trust,"
and doing what's right. ("If in doubt, don't," he cautioned.
"If still in doubt, do what's right.")

So how does this square with his having been the sometimes slippery political operative of the Ford administration, or the ruthless executive whom *Fortune* tagged as one
of "America's Ten Toughest Bosses"?

Is this a case of situational ethics—or is it further evidence that there is more than one "Rumsfeld" out there?

"MR. CLEAN"

It's worth saying again, in the context of this discussion of
moral leadership, that there is no evidence of any wrongdoing at any point in Rumsfeld's career. Note the words
that his critics have used to describe him—for example,
"ruthless within the rules." Robert Hartmann complained
that Rumsfeld's "self-confidence and long-range ambitions
were too conspicuous to conceal." Former Rumsfeld
detractor Henry Kissinger also grumbled about Rummy's
naked ambition—at one Cabinet meeting, he annoyed
Rumsfeld by joking that Rumsfeld's wife had been caught

measuring Kissinger's office—but he used the word "honorable" in describing his old adversary.

If "ruthless within the rules," self-confident, and ambitious are the worst things they say about you, you're doing something right. (And if your adversary calls you "honorable," that's another good sign.) Combine that with an ability to stay far away from even the hint of wrongdoing, and you build an enviable reputation for yourself. In 1977, when *Business Week* announced that Rumsfeld was going to accept the Searle CEO position, the magazine quoted an FDA official as follows: "Obviously, hiring someone like Rumsfeld with his 'Mr. Clean' reputation can't help but help Searle's case."

Even in his most hard-nosed phases, Rumsfeld demonstrated a concern about treating people fairly. One episode from the Ford years illustrates the point. Rumsfeld had left it up to his senior department heads to decide for themselves which Nixon appointees they would keep and which they would fire. The Ford administration was tugged in two directions at once on this front: There was pressure to "clean house" and make it clear that this was a new administration. But many of the Nixon appointees were good at their jobs and helped the wheels of government stay in motion. Meanwhile, *some* of the holdovers in the White House had Watergate connections—but many did not.

So some people stayed, and some people left. Of those who left, some were pushed out the door as a direct result of their Watergate connections. But others left strictly for personal reasons. (The tenure of White House staffers is remarkably short.) The job of announcing which of the Nixon holdovers would stay and which would go fell to Ron Nessen, Ford's often beleaguered press secretary. But Nessen made an error of omission: In making the announcements of who was leaving, he failed to distinguish between the "squeaky clean" departees—those untainted by Watergate—and those who were being pushed out as a direct result of their ties to Watergate.

That had the unfortunate effect of tarnishing images that did not deserve to be tarnished. According to Nessen, Rumsfeld was irate: "Rumsfeld chewed my ass for smearing innocent people with a Watergate taint, [and] I deserved it."

A WAR OF GOOD VERSUS EVIL

The Rumsfeld who became America's twenty-first secretary of defense in January of 2001 was well prepared for the tasks that would soon fall to him. He was technically skilled, having run the Byzantine bureaucracy of the White House staff and having done tours of duty at the head of several large organizations (including the Pentagon itself). But he was also *morally grounded*, and surprisingly willing to discuss complex issues in moral terms.

For example, he sees America's war on terrorism as a "moral war"—a conflict that, for moral reasons, we have no choice but to fight. In taking on the Taliban and al Qaeda (and possibly countries that harbor terrorists, such as Iraq or Iran), he believes he is acting as a moral agent. He is waging war against forces that strive to deny his, and America's, values. While it may sound simplistic, to Rumsfeld, America's battle against terrorism is a case of good versus evil. To that extent, this war closely resembles World War II and the fight against Hitler and Nazism—although he is quick to say that this is a different type of war and cannot be fought like conventional wars of the past.

In his remarks at his official welcoming ceremony in January of 2001, Rumsfeld closed his speech with a com-

ment about "character" that would acquire deeper significance as subsequent events unfolded:

> *I close with a thought that occurred to me as*
> *President Bush spoke on Saturday...about the*
> *qualities that make America special and exceptional.*
> *He talked about civility, courage, character—*
> *reminders that the strength that matters most is not*
> *the strength of arms but the strength of character;*
> *character expressed in service to something larger*
> *than ourselves. And if that is an ultimate safeguard,*
> *then we are indeed a blessed nation.*

Two weeks after the war got under way in Afghanistan,
Rumsfeld addressed the troops at Whiteman Air Force
Base. In simple and powerful terms, he posed a "choice"—
while he argued for America's appropriate role in a post-
September 11th world. Here we get the chance to see how
Rumsfeld, the patriot, becomes Rumsfeld, the pragmatist
(for more on Rumsfeld the pragmatist, see Chapter 11):

> *We have two choices: Either we change the*
> *way we live, or we must change the way they live.*
> *We choose the latter. And you are the ones who*
> *will help achieve that goal.*

He also put terrorists and any other country on notice
that anyone who attacked the United States would pay a
terrible price for their acts of aggression:

> *The terrorists who visited this violence on America*
> *have made a terrible mistake—they have awakened*
> *our nation to a new kind of evil. And in causing this*
> *awakening, they have assured their own destruction.*

> *Out of this act of terror—and the awakening it*
> *brings—here and across the globe—will surely*
> *come a victory over terrorism.*

Can war, which is inescapably based on the killing of people, ever be "moral"? Presumably, the individual who assumes the position of secretary of defense would answer that question in the affirmative. But that still leaves all the various *tactics* of war on the table.

At his briefings, Rumsfeld is often peppered with questions about civilian casualties—a topic with which the Taliban were scoring propaganda points early in the course of the war. Rumsfeld's response? First, he accused the Taliban of lying and of greatly exaggerating the number of innocent civilians who were being killed by American bombs and missiles. Then he went a step further, saying that the blame for any such casualties belongs squarely on the shoulders of those who attacked America in the first place:

> *Is it possible at some point that a civilian was killed?*
> *Yes. We announced here at this podium that a civilian*
> *was killed and it was an accident and unfortunate, and*
> *we regret the loss of any innocent life. But that person*
> *was not killed by us; that person was killed when the al*
> *Qaeda and bin Laden attacked the United States and*
> *killed thousands of people and caused us to have to go*
> *into that country and root out those terrorists before*
> *they kill thousands more. And it's important for the*
> *people of the world to understand that.*

AN AGE OF PARADOXES

As we have seen, secretaries of defense must be willing to wage war—and must be prepared to deal with the moral shadings that arise in the course of prosecuting a war. (Rumsfeld is prepared on both counts.) But most recent heads of the Pentagon, including Rumsfeld, have taken pains to make a corollary argument: If a nation is sufficiently strong, it can *deter* war. If you hate war, in other words, you should love a strong Department of Defense. Here are some relevant excerpts from an Annual Defense Department Report issued by Rumsfeld, in which he makes the case for increased military spending:

> *We live in an age of paradoxes, at a time when hope and peril run side by side. To be just and compassionate, we must be strong. As you consider this budget, you will inevitably consider the military environment, the state of our defenses, and the facts of the world situation, as I have done. The arithmetic is not encouraging; the acts are not kind, but the task is fundamental.*

That report was filed not by America's twenty-first secretary of defense but by its thirteenth secretary of defense—Donald Rumsfeld—during his first tour of duty at the Pentagon. In the late 1970s, America's greatest threat came from the Soviet Union. Today, it comes from a new brand of tyranny, falsely cloaked in the rhetoric of a religion and grossly mislabeled as a "righteous cause." In staring down or taking on either of these adversaries—and others, as they present themselves—Rumsfeld has always believed that fighting to protect the American way of life is a moral cause. He had held, and acted on, the belief that "values have consequences."

Remember the responsibilities of your office: Whether you are running a war or a company, people depend on you—both for your skills and for your moral leadership. Do not shun or underestimate that responsibility.

Live your integrity: Adopt a zero-tolerance policy for ethical lapses. Make it clear to the entire organization that you will not tolerate such lapses. Heed Rumsfeld's advice: Never do or say anything that you do not want to see published on the front page of a newspaper.

Develop a core set of values that all managers and employees can subscribe to: Crafting a set of values can be an important tool in transforming culture in an organization. But understand that cultures are not changed overnight. It can often take years to effect meaningful change in a large organization. In that time period, senior people must lead by example: living the values they espouse.

Never compromise your values: Rumsfeld has stayed true to his values, over many years and several administrations. He has dealt with Cold War foes and the current threat of terrorism. The enemies may have changed, but his commitment to preserving the American ideal has not.

Understand the consequences of your values: Rumsfeld has spoken eloquently on the topic of values and their consequences. Think about the things that you hold dear and why these things are important to you. Understand that your values, beliefs, and actions have consequences.

THE WAR CEO

A New Brand of Leadership

We need to face the reality that the attacks of September 11th—horrific as they were—may in fact be a dim preview of what is to come if we do not prepare today to defend our people from adversaries with weapons of increasing power and range. President Bush is committed to addressing all asymmetric threats.

—DONALD RUMSFELD IN DOD BRIEFING

When I took this job I had a visit with the president shortly thereafter, and we talked about the situation that a lot of the people in the world had come to conclude that the United States was gun-shy....We discussed it and he and I concluded that whenever it occurred down the road that the United States was under some sort of a threat or attack, that the United States would be leaning forward, not back.

—DONALD RUMSFELD, TIME MAGAZINE, DECEMBER 2001

ON THE MORNING of September 11th, Donald Rumsfeld was hosting a breakfast at the Pentagon, using the occasion to lay out a bleak vision of things to come:

I had said at an 8:00 breakfast that sometime in the next two, four, six, eight, ten, twelve months, there would be an event in the world that would be sufficiently shocking that it would remind people how important it is to have a strong, healthy defense department....

Fifteen minutes later, a huge jet smashed into the Pentagon, shaking the building to its foundation and killing more than 180 of Rumsfeld's colleagues. Instinctively, Rumsfeld dashed out of the room, asked if anyone knew what had happened, then ran toward the smoke. Surrounded by chaos and rubble and rescue workers, he helped get some of the wounded onto stretchers.

In interviews later, Rumsfeld downplayed the significance of his actions, implying that anyone in his position would have done the same thing. Maybe so, but Rumsfeld won high marks for his decisive actions that morning. As *The Economist* observed: "He [Rumsfeld] had done what soldiers have to do: stand fast when the world explodes around you. He had led by example."

He certainly had. True, Rumsfeld had had training as a Navy pilot, but those days were nearly half a century behind him. And nothing could have prepared him for the sight of his own "headquarters" building in flames as a result of a fully loaded commercial airliner's plowing into it and igniting it. Simply put, it must have been hell—and Rumsfeld, pushing age seventy, ran into hell and began loading stretchers.

Once he was convinced that the rescue and fire-fighting efforts were well under way, Rumsfeld headed back to his office, figuring it was time to "get at it" (Rumsfeld's way to describe taking command of the situation). One of his first acts was to order Air National Guard fighters into the air to defend both New York and Washington. (It later emerged, however, that the order to shoot down any commercial aircraft that did not respond to communication was suggested by Vice President Cheney and agreed to by President Bush.) Then "he [Rumsfeld] raised the defense-signaling U.S. offensive-readiness to DefCon 3, the highest it had been since the Arab-Israeli war in 1973."

And it was in these fateful minutes—beginning with an unimaginable tragedy and carrying forward into the beginnings of a response to that tragedy—that a seemingly out-of-touch secretary of defense was transformed into a vigorous and vital "secretary of war," with a critical mandate.

RUN *TOWARD* THE PROBLEM

Since those first fateful moments, Rumsfeld has not stopped running in the right direction. With the possible exception of Colin Powell, no other member of the cabinet has received more credit for effectively responding to the initial shock, the ensuing crisis, or the challenge of planning for the longer term. Given the strength of Bush's cabinet, this is no small accomplishment.

Bush's own role and contribution should not be overlooked, especially in a chapter entitled "The War CEO." Bush *is* the nation's CEO, of course, and has done much to provide a vision and set an agenda for the nation in the wake of the terrorist attacks. (His speech before Congress on September 20th, 2001, was a particularly powerful example.) While many had doubts about Bush prior to September 11th, in part due to his razor-thin electoral college margin and his lack of experience in foreign affairs, he found his mandate, and his voice, in the war on terrorism. "What he lacks in experience, he has made up in instinct," declared *Time* in their 2001 year-end story summarizing the first days of the war.

But who is primarily responsible for devising and implementing the U.S. military strategy in Afghanistan? The answer is complex, since many of Bush's closest advisors were involved in crafting the U.S. response from the first hours following the attacks, including Dick Cheney, Colin Powell, Condoleezza Rice, George Tenet (CIA), and Donald Rumsfeld. However, the execution of the strategy falls primarily on the secretary of defense.

Henry Kissinger concurs: "Military strategy of the war against terrorism comes in large part from the Pentagon," he says, "and from my own observation of it the leadership of Rumsfeld is one of the major reasons why it has been so effective and so crisp."

Edward Luttwak, senior fellow at the Center for Strategic Studies, gave President Bush high marks for his handling of the crisis in large part, because he delegated the task of winning the war to Rumsfeld:

You can thus measure Bush as a wartime President by one simple criterion. He basically told the Secretary of Defense, Please fight and please win. He

set no constraints. And by these lights, I rate George
Bush very highly....he has acted right.

In "acting right," Bush thrust his secretary of defense
into the national limelight, to make critical decisions and
answer urgent questions at a time of national crisis. And
while the celebrated Pentagon press briefings have put
Rumsfeld in the spotlight and won him acclaim, there is far
more to Rumsfeld's leadership style than clever quips and
an acid tongue. Earlier chapters have elaborated on some
of the critical building blocks that have contributed to
Rumsfeld's success (e.g., straight talk, moral leadership,
and skilled coalition building). In this chapter, we will go a
step further and develop a general framework with rele-
vance to many different leadership situations. That framework has five parts:

- Lead with vision
- Define and reinforce the mission
- Get the troops to execute the mission
- Build alliances, but control the agenda
- Communicate constantly and clearly

LEAD WITH VISION

As CEO of the Pentagon, and as chief spokesman for the
war, Rumsfeld assumed the front line position in communicating the administration's vision and in getting the
armed forces to execute that vision. President Bush had
declared war on terrorists and terrorism and also decreed
that any countries that harbored terrorists would find no
safe haven. Rumsfeld also took a large measure of respon-

sibility for keeping Americans informed of key develop-
ments on waging this new war. And all of this started with
a *vision*.

Rumsfeld's vision for the military was formed long before
September 11th. Significantly, it was a vision based on
change—often the biggest challenge of the chief executive
officer. In late January of 2001, for example, Rumsfeld spoke
of "continuing change" and of the importance of grasping
certain new realities in order to make Americans safe:

> *The state of change that we see in our military world*
> *may well be the new status quo. We may not be in the*
> *process of transition to something that will follow the*
> *Cold War. Rather, we may be in a period of*
> *continuing change, and if so, the sooner we wrap*
> *our heads around the fact, the sooner we can get*
> *about the business of making this nation and its*
> *citizens as safe and secure as they must be in*
> *our new national security environment.*

Few paid much attention to Rumsfeld back then. Many
dismissed him as a relic of a long-gone (and demonstrably
ineffective) administration. However, there was at least one
individual who believed that the new defense secretary was
on to something with all this talk of change—and that individual was President Bush. Several months prior to the
attacks, in a frank discussion with the president, Rumsfeld
had spoken of how America was seen as "gun-shy" and
"risk averse" and of how important it would be to alter
that perception should something happen that required
military action:

> *I left no doubt in his mind that, at that moment*
> *where something happens, that I would be coming to*

him to lean forward, not back. And that I wanted
[him] to know that. And he [President Bush] said
unambiguously, that this is what we would be doing,
and we had a clear common understanding.

So Rumsfeld, working in public and private, and working both up and down the chain of command, already had laid the groundwork for what was to come. In fact, he had warned about the threat of "rogue nations" and "asymmetrical threats" for years and had advocated an overhaul of the military precisely to deal with those new types of threats. Unfortunately, it took the tragedies of September 11th to prove him right.

DEFINE AND REINFORCE THE MISSION

On the day after the attacks, Rumsfeld briefed reporters and the American public and delivered the "new battlefield" speech cited in earlier chapters (Chapters 1 and 3). "We are, in a sense, seeing the definition of a new battlefield in the world, a twenty-first-century battlefield, and it is a different kind of conflict." In answering questions on that day, he spoke of the terrorist attacks as "an attack on a way of life." In sharp contrast to the briefings from other recent wars, in this case he prepared the nation for a long, drawn-out military affair:

Anyone who thinks it's easy is wrong. I think that it
will require a sustained and broadly based effort. And
I don't think that people ought to judge outcomes
until a sufficient time has passed to address what is
clearly a very serious problem for the world. And it's
not restricted to a single entity, state, or non-state
entity. It is an attack on a way of life.

Rumsfeld hammered away at these themes in his briefings. In late September, he also published a piece in the *New York Times* articulating some themes seldom heard from a leader of the Pentagon:

> *Some people believe that the first casualty of any war is the truth. But in this war, the first victory must be to tell the truth....This is not a war against an individual, a group, a religion or a country....Even the vocabulary will be different....Forget about 'exit strategies'; we're looking at a sustained engagement that carries no deadlines. We have no fixed rules about how to deploy our troops.*

These public pronouncements had several effects. First, of course, they set the stage for preparing the public for the war in Afghanistan that would start in early October. But just as important, they helped establish a rapport with the press corps—and by extension, the nation—that would have to come to understand a new kind of war in "real time."

GET THE TROOPS TO EXECUTE THE MISSION

On the same day that he conducted his first formal post-attack briefing (September 12th), Rumsfeld also addressed U.S. forces and Department of Defense civilians. This was the speech that invoked the name of Churchill and reminded his listeners that "great crises are defined by memorable moments." He spoke of how the tragedy brought on one of "the finest hours" at the Pentagon and then spoke of the importance of "vanquishing" the enemies:

> *The task of vanquishing these terrible enemies and in protecting the American people and the cause of*

human freedom will fall to you....I know we are ready. I know America can continue to count on your selflessness and courage and dedication to duty. Let us never forget what this great institution is about....Heroes have gone before us. Here at the Pentagon yesterday, heroes were here again.

Rumsfeld's efforts to "rally the troops" extended literally to the troops themselves, of course. In the final months of 2001, he made several speeches designed to get the men and women of the armed services fully motivated and battle-ready. In late November, for example, he addressed the soldiers assembled at Fort Bragg, North Carolina:

You're part of an organization that requires you to prove yourselves over and over again. You do it in training, and you do it when you're deployed. Strong backs, that's for sure—I've shaken some big strong hands today—but also strong hearts, strong minds as well....On behalf of the President, the Department of Defense, the American people, I thank you....I thank you for all you do to keep America free. We value and we respect your courage and your determination and your dedication.

One noteworthy individual who praises Rumsfeld's management of the war is Henry Kissinger: "I think his performance is outstanding. And I am a tremendous admirer of the way he is organizing the defense deparment—he has driven the military operations that are taking place—and the contribution he's making to national strategy and finally the enormous public education that he's undertaken."

BUILD ALLIANCES, BUT CONTROL THE AGENDA

From the outset, it was clear to Bush and his cabinet that one of the keys to winning this new and unorthodox war was to build an alliance of nations that would assist the United States in a variety of ways. These would include, for example, giving the United States access to military bases, providing intelligence, rounding up al Qaeda operatives and other suspected terrorists, and freezing the assets of suspected terrorist organizations.

George Bush, Colin Powell, and to a lesser extent Dick Cheney spent many weeks putting together such a coalition and then trying to keep it strong and functioning. Although there had been wartime coalitions in the past—including the one that the first President Bush put together to help prosecute the Gulf War—this particular alliance was unprecedented. Each of its members had strong opinions about what a "war on terrorism" meant, and some of those opinions didn't fit together particularly well. ("One man's terrorist is another man's freedom fighter.") Most nations that signed up with the coalition made it clear that their cooperation came with qualifications. For example, Powell had to report to the president that if the U.S. military effort ventured beyond Afghanistan, Saudi Arabia and Egypt would most likely pull out.

Rumsfeld grasped the complexity of the situation. On September 12th, in a meeting with Bush and his advisors, Rumsfeld weighed in on the importance of defining the goals precisely right out of the starting gate: "It is critical how we define goals at the start, because that's what the coalition signs on for. Other countries want precise definitions. Do we focus on bin Laden and al Qaeda or terrorism more broadly?"

Bush responded unflinchingly: "Start with bin Laden."

Although much of the burning up of phone lines was left to others (chiefly Colin Powell), it is clear that Rumsfeld played a vital role in the behind-the-scenes strategy sessions on building the coalition. Later he warned against allowing the coalition to control the agenda. This was a vital point to Rumsfeld. He knew that it was absolutely critical for the U.S. to set and maintain the agenda. Any other course of action would diminish America's ability to accomplish its mission.

However, in making sure the coalition stayed solid and together, Rumsfeld didn't always remain in the shadows. In early December, some two months into the war, Rumsfeld made a whirlwind trip around the Middle East in order to allay fears and quiet the nerves of coalition members. He made stops in Saudi Arabia, Egypt, and Oman before heading on to Uzbekistan (home to a base that might be a key resource for future U.S. military actions). The internal politics of these nations are as thorny as any in the world, and their relations to the United States are greatly complicated by U.S. support for Israel in the long-running Israeli-Palestinian struggle.

Another member of the Bush cabinet could have gone on this vital diplomatic tour, of course, but it was the ex-NATO ambassador who was asked to make the trip. Rumsfeld was charged with taking the American argument directly to the Arab world. Interviewed on Pakistani television, for example, he spoke at length on the role of the coalition, why the United States was bombing Afghanistan, and why that course of action was justified. He also made it quite clear that the Bush administration would deal in similar fashion with any country that attacked us:

Our interest is in working with other countries to stop
terrorists from killing people. Our only interest in
Afghanistan is to deal with the al Qaeda and to

*change the leadership in Afghanistan so that there is a
stable, broadly based government....So our effort is
an effort in self-defense. What we're engaged in is an
effort to prevent terrorists—these terrorists or other
terrorists—from thinking that they can with impunity
use weapons of mass destruction, because they can't.
We're going to stop them.*

COMMUNICATE CONSTANTLY AND CLEARLY

In times of uncertainty, people like to be kept informed up
to the minute of pertinent events. As discussed in previous
chapters, one of Rumsfeld's strengths is the way he manages the dissemination of information: he is often candid,
but is careful not to give out any information that (1) may
prove to be wrong or (2) may put American lives in harm's
way. In part because of his determination not to repeat the
mistakes of past wars, he became one of the most able
communicators in the history of U.S. secretaries of defense.

The ability to communicate candidly, and in a manner
that builds trust and rapport, is a hallmark of great leaders.
Franklin Roosevelt was one of the twentieth century's most
effective political communicators, and one of the keys to
his success was his ability to connect with the American
people. Through his "fireside chats," which took full
advantage of the power of radio, he created a powerful
sense of intimacy with millions of Americans. He used this
unprecedented relationship to explain, first, his measures
to combat the Great Depression and, subsequently, the
Allied cause against fascism. In fact, he never stopped
explaining why the war was important and had to be won.

Rumsfeld, too, has used a powerful medium to forge a
bond with millions of Americans. Record numbers of people regularly tune in to his televised press briefings. When

Time magazine named New York Mayor Rudolph Giuliani its "Person of the Year" in December of 2001, NBC conducted a poll to determine the "people's choice" for person of the year. That poll indicated that Rumsfeld would have come in fifth had the question been put to a popular vote. Fifth place is not first place, of course—but given the fact that few Americans could have identified him before September 11th, Rumsfeld has clearly had a powerful impact on the national consciousness.

THE RUMSFELD WAY

Run toward the problem: When Rumsfeld ran toward the horrific scene at the Pentagon on September 11th, he was leading by example. Few leaders will experience such a terrible context for leadership, of course, but all should "run toward the problem."

Lead with vision: Long before the war started, Rumsfeld had articulated his vision for a new approach to national defense. He had talked about a period of continuous change and about the need to develop security measures against "rogue nations" and terrorism.

Define and reinforce the mission: Within one day of the attacks, Rumsfeld was communicating the mission—to rid the world of terrorism so that the American way of life could continue to flourish. He addressed every audience to which he had access: the press, Pentagon staffers, members of the armed forces, and the public (both through the press and through his own writings). He hammered his key points home time and again in the opening months of the war on terrorism.

Get the troops to execute: Rumsfeld has achieved celebrity status by serving as "Articulator in Chief." Meanwhile, he has kept in mind that as Pentagon CEO, his role is to build the morale of the troops. He has made several trips to bases and also to Afghanistan to stand side by side with the soldiers who have been called upon to defend the nation's interests in faraway (and dangerous) places.

Build alliances, but control the agenda: Coalition building has been a key, but Rumsfeld recognized from the beginning that the United States must not let its allies control the strategy or agenda. That would risk making the offensive less effective.

Never stop communicating: Great leaders understand that they must be great communicators. Prior to September 11th, no one would have nominated Rumsfeld as a masterful communicator. But by the end of 2001, he and his briefings had become one of the most talked-about "shows" on television. He has also used his "bully pulpit" to continuously explain *why* America is at war, thus building and maintaining support for America's military effort.

ACQUIRING AND USING INTELLIGENCE

Gain Knowledge and Make It Work

*In any large organization, there is always the need
to reach down and know how things are really
functioning. You need to know you're getting the
truth, hearing the bad news as well as the good.*
DONALD RUMSFELD, FORTUNE, SEPTEMBER 1979

When taking over a troubled company, a knowledgeable CEO checks his or her teeth to tail ratio, as they say in the military. It involves a thorough undertaking of the company's assets and resources....This forces the company to focus on its core business and to avoid wasting manpower, time, and money on ventures that are secondary to what is vital to the long-term health and success of the company.

—DONALD RUMSFELD, JUNE 1995

WHILE RUMSFELD WAS PONDERING a potential move to the chief executive's office at G. D. Searle, many of his friends were telling him that it was a terrible idea. Searle was in dire straits. It had a tarnished reputation in Washington, especially among the regulators who had enormous power over its fortunes. And although Rumsfeld's relationship with the Searle chief went back some fifteen years—Searle had provided key support for a successful Rumsfeld congressional bid—Rumsfeld knew little about the pharmaceutical business.

But Rumsfeld took the job nevertheless. There were several reasons. The money certainly had some appeal, but—as he later said—compensation "wasn't the deciding factor." (His Searle salary began at about $450,000, not including a generous stock-option package.) The real appeal, Rumsfeld subsequently explained, was getting an opportunity outside of Washington to do something "big" and "challenging." He wanted a context where his actions could have an immediate effect on the bottom line:

What I was looking for, was something
outside of Washington I could get fully
engaged in, something I could become central to.
What I wanted was something big, complex and
international enough to be challenging.

"Don Rumsfeld likes nothing better than an impossible task," proclaimed Bryce Harlow, a top White House official in the Eisenhower and Nixon administrations. "He took the Searle job almost defiantly to show he could do an impossible job."

GATHER INTELLIGENCE BEFORE YOU START

Once he decided to take the Searle job in April, Rumsfeld had three months before his official starting date in June. He was determined not to come into the job uninformed. Between April and June, he spent as much time as he could learning the business:

I decided to do it, starting in June.
I spent the intervening period talking
to people, accumulating different
perspectives on what was working well
and what might need attention.

In other words, Rumsfeld began his knowledge-gathering effort months before going on the payroll. Judging by how quickly he was able to turn the company around, the way Rumsfeld spent those three months appears to have been critical. He got up to speed on the crucial issues and planned his opening moves.

One of his first moves was to establish five task forces consisting of directors, managers, and outsiders. He took pains to ensure that each task force included a wide spectrum of voices and organized each of the groups around one of the five key areas that he defined as most critical to the company's future: finance, government compliance, scientific research, cost control, and global competition. Rumsfeld made sure to involve the troika (the three executives who were still in positions of power) in this agenda-setting process as well.

The task forces helped Rumsfeld get a handle on what was working and what wasn't. Rumsfeld believed that companies often try to do too much—acquiring too many businesses, launching too many new initiatives, and so on. In *Rumsfeld's Rules*, he recommends that companies limit their initiatives and actively "prune" the businesses, processes, and positions that don't add value to the business.

Rumsfeld evidently came to the Searle job with this mindset. He soon found, however, he had his work cut out for him. The company he inherited was in a severe need of an overhaul.

NEW BLOOD, "NEW LEADERSHIP CENTERS"

Bringing Rumsfeld aboard sparked several management changes from the outset. The troika that had been running the company all got new jobs and titles. Daniel Searle, who had been chief executive for 13 years, moved up to chairman. His brother William and his brother-in-law Wesley Dixon both became vice chairmen. All three were impressed at how quickly their new CEO immersed himself in the business, and—by involving them in each step of the change process—Rumsfeld earned the authority to go forward.

Rumsfeld determined that in addition to the company's sagging earnings, Searle's most pressing problems were the result of misjudgments and missteps. Searle had a rocky relationship with the Food and Drug Administration, the federal agency that largely controlled the fortunes of Searle and its competitors. The company also was facing a Justice Department investigation into the possible falsification of drug test results on two antihypertensive (blood pressure) medications. The company's other problems included a failed diversification strategy and a research pipeline that had gone dry—over the long run, a fatal shortcoming for a drug company.

Rumsfeld had already established a reputation for "my-way-or-the-highway" ruthlessness. Nevertheless, he knew that success depended on putting together a team that could help him address the company's key problems. To assist in his turnaround efforts, he brought in new blood that would help him solve several of the critical problems that were plaguing the company. Fortunately, his tough-guy image did not prevent him from assembling a first-rate team.

> *They say I use the stick and not the carrot.*
> *The truth is I use both.*

To create what Rumsfeld called "multiple leadership centers" at Searle, the new chief hired a team of similarly hard-charging executives in their forties and fifties who shared his relentless work ethic. His management philosophy for building teams was the simplest conceivable one:

> *It's always been my philosophy to*
> *hire the best and get out of the way.*

Rumsfeld felt that the team he assembled fit the bill. Long-time friend John Robson, a former chairman of the Civil Aeronautics Board, was brought in to help Rumsfeld navigate the regulatory issues. He also brought in seasoned financial executive James M. Kenney to serve as CFO. Another of Rumsfeld's hiring coups involved recruiting Dr. Daniel Azarnoff, a renowned professor of medicine and pharmacology.

Azarnoff turned out to be the key to turning around Searle's lackluster R&D effort. Most interesting about this hire was the fact that other companies had tried and failed to recruit Azarnoff in the past. It was "the way Rumsfeld went about it" that convinced him to take the offer, Azarnoff later explained. "My reaction was quite different than when headhunters called." Evidently, Rumsfeld was a highly effective salesman when it came to sketching a vision and building a team.

Rumsfeld also moved to restructure the board, feeling that it included too many company insiders. The newly assembled team included a number of prominent outside-world executives, former government officials, and medical authorities. When the restructuring was complete, only four of the fifteen board members were Searle employees. This move—which surely involved enormous amounts of internal politicking and maneuvering—helped the company begin the transition from a paternalistic family-run business to a more professionally managed company.

RUMSFELD'S "BAD NEWS" POLICY

Once the Rumsfeld team was in place, it began working to address the company's ailing business portfolio and mounting financial problems. Just as important to Rumsfeld, though, was instituting a number of measures to help the company manage and respond to the kinds of ethical and quality issues that got it into deep trouble in the first place.

One of the most visible measures Rumsfeld took was implementing what he called a "bad news" policy. The intent of the new policy was to make sure that top management became aware of product and performance issues much faster than had been the case in the past.

This tactic was, in some ways, ahead of its time. It would get far more press in the 1990s, when CEOs like Andy Grove and Bill Gates began writing on the subject. Grove, for example, told managers to "listen to Cassandras" in his book, *Only the Paranoid Survive*, and urged executives to make sure that they had a way of getting bad news from all corners of the company. In his second book (*Business @ the Speed of Thought*), Bill Gates wrote of the importance of "a digital nervous system" to ensure that all managers and employees share and have access to vital information.

But Rumsfeld—no doubt prompted by his experience in Washington, where bad news seems to travel at the speed of light—came up with his own early warning system years before other business leaders made it such a prominent part of their own agendas.

NEW STANDARDS FOR A NEW IMAGE

Rumsfeld also took other decisive measures to address the ills of the company. According to Joseph McCann, author of *Sweet Success* (the book that detailed Rumsfeld's turn-around of Searle and the creation of NutraSweet), several other key measures were instituted in order to repair the company's tarnished image on the quality and ethics fronts:

> *Rigorous documentation and research protocols were instituted as part of the quality assurance program. A corporate-wide standards of conduct policy was created to visibly emphasize Searle's ethical business practices.*

By adding research protocols and strict companywide ethics standards, Rumsfeld was sending a vital message: This was not the same company that had allegedly rigged drug results data. By extension, this was not a company destined to repeat the mistakes of the past.

McCann described other key Rumsfeld decisions that played a vital role in helping to put the company on the road to recovery:

New financial controls and information systems had been introduced to support more decentralized management. Financial performance began improving dramatically after the first two years of restructuring.

Several of these early Rumsfeld moves were clearly cutting-edge: For example, few CEOs were talking about the importance of decentralized management in the late 1970s, nor were they talking about "hiring the best and getting out of the way." The fact that these new philosophies were articulated and embraced by a CEO with almost no business experience makes them all the more impressive.

In this context, it is impossible to recount all the thousands of decisions, large and small, that helped effect the turnaround at Searle. In addition to the steps already mentioned, these included a massive restructuring of the business portfolio (mostly divesting non-drug businesses), a recasting of the expense structure through the elimination of the majority of the corporate staff, an aggressive drug licensing strategy, and systems aimed at tackling the difficult decisions as quickly as possible.

Rumsfeld has always said that in the end, it is *results that count*. At Searle, Rumsfeld got results, turning a floundering and unfocused company into a highly profitable firm with a solid reputation. In 1982, Lawrence Smith—an analyst who had closely followed the company—afforded Rumsfeld high praise for his leadership:

He forced each division to adhere to rigorous control mechanisms to meet growth goals. He is decisive, a good motivator, good at hiring and strong at firing.

WINNING THE INTELLIGENCE WAR

The September 11th debacle was one of the worst intelligence failures in history (although that was denied by CIA chief Tenet in his congressional testimony in mid-February of 2002). Winning the "intelligence war" therefore became a top priority, along with winning the war on the ground in Afghanistan. The Defense Department (along with the traditional intelligence agencies) focused on gathering intelligence and using that information to fight the war on terrorism on every front.

In a department of defense briefing in mid-January of 2002, Rumsfeld's opening statements emphasized that the U.S. was rigorously pursuing every shred of data that might help America and its allies:

We continue to conduct intelligence-gathering operations, combing through the tunnels, caves, bunkers, houses, terrorist camps, and interrogating detainees, searching for information that will help us disrupt terrorist networks and prevent further terrorist acts.

The key, said Rumsfeld, was to evaluate every computer, every document, and every last bit of evidence to make sure that the United States learned of any plans for additional terrorist acts that might involve weapons of mass destruction. (It should be noted, however, that examining computers and documents is more of a domestic issue and, therefore, comes under the auspices of the FBI with an assist from the CIA.) In any event, Rumsfeld was convinced that the information that was being gathered in Afghanistan was not only helping to win that war but also arming America against future attacks:

*And towards that end, it is of great urgency that we
access all of the intelligence information that we can.
These are the suspected weapons of mass destruction
sites that we've been examining, Taliban and al Qaeda
safe houses, looking for documents, computers, and
the like, as well as the information and materials that
we're obtaining from the interrogation of now
hundreds of detainees. It's from these activities that
we are most likely to gain the information that will
help us prevent future attacks.*

USE INTELLIGENCE, BUT DON'T REVEAL ALL

The questioning in that same January briefing soon turned
to reports from the island nation of Singapore, where intelligence allegedly had already been used to head off terrorist attacks. (Video and audio evidence from Singapore
showed evidence of a planned attack against U.S. interests
there.) Rumsfeld was asked about that situation and the
specificity and value of that intelligence. From the
exchange, it is apparent that Rumsfeld was privately
briefed on the Singapore situation but did not then know
how much had been reported or what was appropriate for
him to reveal. This was a common circumstance in a
Rumsfeld briefing, and it sounded like this:

Q: *Mr. Secretary, you've spent a lot of time today
talking in your statement about the amount of intelligence that you've gathered. Can you tell us what
role that played in the arrests in Singapore? Was this
one of the success stories of this operation? And
what was the nature of the threat in Singapore
against U.S. military interests that was apparently
thwarted? Can you tell us anything about that?*

RUMSFELD: *Well, I apologize that I've not had a chance today to see television, but I understand that there are some things being said by the Singapore government about the fact that they have rolled up a network or a number of people who were—are suspected of having been terrorists of some sort. And I don't know what else they've said, and I am—I know the answer to your question, but it's not clear that it's for me to get into it.*

Q: *They said that it was—that they caught these people because of a tape that was found in an al Qaeda leader's house in Afghanistan.*

RUMSFELD: *Who said that, the government of Singapore?*

Q: *The government of Singapore.*

RUMSFELD: *Well, if the government of Singapore said that, I'd go with it.*

The questioning moved on to other topics, but eventually returned to the situation in Singapore:

Q: *—how specific the threat was to U.S. forces in Singapore. Could you talk about that?*

RUMSFELD: *It was specific.*

Q: *Well, could you elaborate on that?*

RUMSFELD: *Well, no, I could, but I don't think I should. I mean, there's no question but—I mean, there's going to be—obviously, these people are going to be tried and—or correction—they're going to be interrogated, and then to the extent charges are appropriate, charges will be filed; to the extent charges are filed, they'll be tried, according to Singapore law, one would think. And I don't know that I should get into it.*

This, once again, is vintage Rumsfeld. He understands that the press and the public have a right to know, yet he is careful never to say anything that might compromise lives or missions—or for that matter, steal the thunder of friendly governments. Rumsfeld emphasized that point time after time as he faced the probing press corps:

> **RUMSFELD:** *Let me just take a minute and say something about the intelligence information.*
>
> *If I stood up here and told you precisely that in city X we found item X or Y and are accessing it, it would tell anyone out there that there's a likelihood that we now know something that we previously didn't know that could put them in jeopardy. There are those who are so pleased with all that we're gathering that they're anxious to say what they're gathering, and they're anxious to say the numbers of things we've gathered and what locations we've gathered them from and who gathered them.*
>
> *I'm not. I am much more interested in stopping terrorists. And to the extent that laying all of that out is going to make us look like we're good gatherers, it does not—it does not begin to weigh as much as having us be good and successful in stopping terrorists from killing people.*

That may be the most important lesson of all, when it comes to gathering and using intelligence, particularly in times of crisis and war. In most circumstances, information has to be used in a way that doesn't reveal *how* you know what you know—and thereby protects those sources for the future.

Gather information early: Even before going on the Searle payroll, Rumsfeld spent three months gathering vital information. This proved to be a vital step in helping to bring about a thoroughgoing turnaround. Rumsfeld repeated this policy throughout this career in both business and government. Remember, there is never a moment to lose in today's ultra-competitive environment.

Once you have the necessary data, jump in with both feet: Rumsfeld said he took the Searle CEO job to be "fully engaged and not peripherally involved." He wanted to make a real impact on the company, where he could see the direct results of his actions. Take a page from his book, and do not dabble. If you are going to do something, make a total commitment to the task at hand.

Hire the best and get out of the way: One of the reasons Rumsfeld was so successful was that he surrounded himself with a team of hard-charging managers who shared both his values and his unyielding work ethic. By bringing in such competent people, he was able to focus on the big picture, while others helped with the day-to-day challenges of running the company.

Decentralize: Rumsfeld created "multiple leadership centers" to make his company less bureaucratic, less hierarchical, and less centralized. He was able to do this in part because he had a cadre of capable business leaders at his side.

Get bad news quickly: Most big problems begin as little ones. Make sure that there is a mechanism in place that allows top managers to get access to bad news quickly.

MASTERING THE AGENDA

Set a Strategic Direction

It is useful to ask whether you are working off your 'in' basket or whether the organization is working off your 'out' basket. If it's the former, you may be reacting rather than leading the organization toward agreed-upon priorities.

—DONALD RUMSFELD, SEPTEMBER 1979

*In the grand sweep of history, great leadership
has always been strategic. The essence of strategic
leadership is the process of examining events in
their many dimensions, testing immediate issues in
the context of broader long-term goals, establishing
priorities based on balance among importance,
urgency, and achievability—and then pursuing
policies in the nearer term aimed at securing
the long-range objectives.*

—DONALD RUMSFELD, MAY 1988

ONE RUMSFELD CONSTANT throughout his career has been his *intensity*. In his days with the Nixon and Ford administrations, his work ethic was almost legendary. He evidently saw no reason to change his ways when he got to Searle. After Rumsfeld's arrival at the once low-key pharmaceutical company, office suites were buzzing by 7:00 A.M. and twelve-hour days became the routine. And—as noted in earlier chapters—he ruled with an iron fist, dressing down and firing people at will.

Despite his tough tactics, though, Rumsfeld also has been a thoughtful student of what some may perceive as "softer" subjects, such as values and leadership. In his final year at Searle, for example, Rumsfeld summed up his notion of the essence of leadership:

> *The essential quality of leadership is the courage to decide, to set a direction.*

Perhaps Rumsfeld's statement sounds obvious, or even simplistic. But the fact is that in today's lightning-paced environment, many CEOs have faltered because they hesitated, taking too long to select a course of action for their organization.

When Rumsfeld took the helm at Searle, the company was in desperate need of a leader who could set the agenda, and point the company in the right direction. Rumsfeld soon proved that he could do both of those things.

THE FIRST MOVES ARE KEY

By the time of Rumsfeld's arrival on the scene, Searle had become a slow-moving and unwieldy organization. In the late 1960s and 1970s, the company had gone on a buying spree that contributed to its downward spiral. Searle had acquired more than a dozen companies in a wide variety of fields, including nuclear instrumentation, medical electronics, and veterinary and agricultural products. Not surprisingly, expenses were exploding. In 1977, Searle reported a $95-million write-off, while return on equity had dropped from 50 percent to 11 percent.

Rumsfeld realized that a major restructuring was desperately needed. One of *Rumsfeld's Rules* recommends that companies "prune" annually, ridding themselves of the products, people, and processes that no longer add value. The new CEO took his own advice. In short order, he divested twenty-three businesses worth about $250 million and eliminated more than half of the corporate staff (reducing it from 800 to 350). He also set up a $21 million reserve for a then-moribund saccharin replacement sweetener called *aspartame*. Even though the company had shelled out hundreds of millions developing the drug, which had gone through years of testing, the FDA had still failed to approve its use. Still, Rumsfeld saw much potential in the future of aspartame.

Years later, other CEOs would win acclaim for the type of decisive acts that Rumsfeld had implemented in the late 1970s and early 1980s. However, as mentioned previously, Searle was simply not on the radar screen as one of the world's premier companies, so few outside of Chicago lauded Rumsfeld the CEO. But those actions were nonetheless bold. They effectively reversed many of the significant actions taken by former CEO Daniel Searle and his fellow troika members—even as the troika was still looking over Rumsfeld's shoulder. Selling off those twenty-three businesses was a tacit admission that the company's diversification efforts had failed utterly.

Even so, it was Daniel Searle who gave Rumsfeld the highest marks: "His energy, both mental and physiological, is immense, and that spreads through the entire organization," he explained to the *Wall Street Journal* in 1980. "I'm terribly proud of what Don Rumsfeld has done with the company." And the results certainly back up Daniel Searle's praise. Sales and profits were both up by more than 20 percent in 1980 (excluding the aspartame reserve), and the *Chicago Tribune* was crowing over the Rumsfeld turnaround: "The result has been an about-face at the once ailing, overextended, and family-run company."

DEFINING THE CORE BUSINESS

In order to get things back on track and set a new, profitable agenda, Rumsfeld needed to make sure that everyone knew what Searle's core business really was (pharmaceuticals). Keep in mind that by the time Rumsfeld had arrived, the company's failing diversification efforts had significantly clouded the picture, adding more than a dozen disparate businesses. According to Rumsfeld,

> *The first task is to decide what the core business is. Once this decision is made, everything else is secondary.*

To this extent, Rumsfeld embodied and to some degree anticipated cutting-edge corporate strategic thinking in the

1980s and 1990s. By then, leading executives and business school professors had come to recognize the fundamental flaw in the "conglomerate thinking" that had dominated U.S. industry through much of the 1960s and 1970s. Simply put, that view held that a well-run company can "manage anything" and that diversification into any field, no matter how remote from the core business, was a short-cut to profits.

The approach led hundreds of large firms down dead-end paths. The massive merger-and-acquisition wave of the 1980s was fueled in large part by overdiversified firms spinning off their mistakes. The hard lesson they learned through this experience was to focus on "core competencies," and especially to build on strengths in R&D, manu-facturing, and marketing. Rumsfeld's strategy at Searle was a textbook case of this focused approach.

Deciding on a core business may sound like a simple task, but there are plenty of examples around to suggest otherwise. In some cases, the core business may be a sig-nificant recasting of a traditional field of endeavor. For example, one of the keys to Lou Gerstner's dramatic turn-around of IBM was deciding that IBM was not simply a maker of computers but a broad provider of information technology *solutions*. This opened the door to all sorts of new opportunities and helped bring about the firm's $13-billion turnaround in the late 1990s.

Another example is Jack Welch's makeover of GE. When he took over, the company confidently saw itself as one of the world's premier manufacturing companies. But Welch was restless with what he saw and launched an ambitious and disruptive process of transformation. And in the process of recreating the company, he turned it into one of the world's largest *service* organizations.

RESTRUCTURING FOR GROWTH

Rumsfeld knew that the company needed a structure that could help it to focus on its core business. He therefore divided his unwieldy organization into three major group segments. The largest was the core pharmaceutical/consumer products group, which was responsible for the majority of the company's sales and profits. (Sales in 1979 exceeded half a billion dollars, with $149 million in operating earnings.) The second group was the medical products group, the third the optical products group.

Rumsfeld suspected that Searle's future lay in its pharmaceutical/consumer products group. In fact, Rumsfeld saw the potential for doubling sales in that market segment within four years, and possibly less. The consumer products segment within that group was growing so rapidly that it was made into a separate unit with its own general manager, whom Rumsfeld had hired away from a division of Mattel.

Divesting lagging businesses, downsizing the company, amassing a seasoned management team, and focusing on the core business—all were key tactics in bringing about the turnaround of Searle. And they were tactics that would prove useful at a later point in Rumsfeld's career, when the stakes were immensely higher.

CRAFTING AN AGENDA ON
"MISSION AND MINDSET"

In the United States, unlike the case in many parts of the world, the military cannot act independently but must answer to civilian political leaders—most notably the commander in chief, Congress (which formally votes on declarations of war), and ultimately the American people. As a practical matter, however, the decision to go to war rests most heavily on the shoulders of the President and his closest advisors. They possess the highest-level military intelligence about real or potential armed conflicts, and they communicate and negotiate with other world leaders. And sooner or later, they must "sell" their decisions—including the usually unpopular decision to go to war—to the voting public.

For the last of these reasons, democratic leaders face greater challenges in times of national emergency than despots, who have the luxury of being able to act unilaterally and without public approval. American leaders not only must win the war on the battlefield but must also win—as President Woodrow Wilson put it during World War I—"the war for the American mind."

To the extent that a crisis can be anticipated, the battle for the American mind must be joined in advance. And even before he had formal responsibility for doing so, Rumsfeld was focusing public attention on national security and the existence of new threats. In 1998, for example, he headed a commission that pointed to threats from rogue states such as Iran and Iraq. The Rumsfeld Commission received a great deal of attention, particularly from the Republican right, due to its controversial findings and recommendations.

In March of that same year, Rumsfeld addressed the conservative Heritage Foundation in a speech entitled "Strategic Imperatives in East Asia." In a well-articulated argument, Rumsfeld spoke of the importance of pursuing a strong, unambiguous, and serious foreign policy in order to protect U.S. interests around the world. He proclaimed this particularly important in an age that "lacks the defining clarity":

At home, uncertainty leads to confusion, and with it a lack of resolve. To our allies it represents unreliability; to our enemies, weakness. It invites miscalculation. And in this era when weapons of mass

*destruction are spreading so insidiously and so
invidiously, miscalculation invites disaster. Just as
military weakness provocatively tempts others into
adventures they would otherwise avoid, uncertainty
and unpredictability in foreign policy are provocative
in the same way and for the same reason.*

Those words seem particularly prescient in the wake of
September 11th. Clearly, the Taliban and al Qaeda "mis-
calculated" when they assumed that the United States
would not respond to the planned attacks with massive
military force—a well-crafted plan that that would put
American soldiers on the ground in Afghanistan.

In his official welcoming ceremony as secretary of
defense in January of 2001, Rumsfeld found yet another
opportunity to speak of the new perils facing the United
States. He also reiterated his sense of urgency in making
sure that America was ready to deal with and counter those
new threats. He began by reiterating the stated goals of his
new boss:

*President Bush takes office with three goals in mind:
to strengthen the bond of trust with the American
military, to protect the American people both from
attack and threats of terror, and to build a military
that takes advantage of remarkable new technologies
to confront the new threats of this century.*

Rumsfeld went on to speak about the need for a new
sense of urgency, stressing that it was critically important
not to wait for things to "shake out" before taking action:

*Reaching those [President Bush's] goals is a matter of
mission and of mindset. Among the things we must*

combat is a sense that we have all the time in the world to get to the task that's at hand. There's a sense out there that we can't or we needn't act, because the world is changing; that we're in a transition period between the Cold War and the next era, whatever it may be; and that we can wait until things shake out and settle down a bit.

In addition to changing "mission" and "mindset," how would Rumsfeld hope to achieve the goals of a more secure America? One of the keys to his vision was to dramatically increase defense spending. (This was true even before September 11th.) In early 2002, Rumsfeld explained that given the size of the American armed forces, it usually takes five years or more to make a significant impact on the vast machinery that is the American military. (In 2002 the U.S. armed forces numbered 1.4 million, with another 1.3 million troops in the reserves. An additional 300,000 civilians were also on the payroll.)

DECISION MAKING AND THE PATH TO WAR

In the days that followed the terrorist attacks, President George W. Bush met round the clock with his key advisors—first on September 12th in the White House Situation Room and subsequently at Camp David.

Time reported that "everything was on the table at Camp David when the war council gathered on September 15th." (That group generally consisted of Vice President Cheney, Secretary of Defense Rumsfeld, Secretary of State Powell, National Security Advisor Condoleezza Rice, Chairman of the Joint Chiefs Shelton, and CIA Director George Tenet.) The magazine also quoted an unnamed official at the meeting who said that most agreed on committing troops to a ground assault in Afghanistan:

There was the discussion of boots on the ground.
Pretty quickly, most everybody thinks you've gotta do
it, you've gotta show that level of seriousness.

The next day, Bush fired off a number of key decisions to National Security Advisor Rice, which included his vision for the war on terrorism. The war would, at least in the initial phase, be limited to Afghanistan. The President also laid out the strategy of an intense aerial campaign, combined with the use of military special forces and military commandos. With this strategy laid out, planning began, and the war commenced with air strikes in early October. Although there was talk of a potential "quagmire"—with the specter of American troops' getting stuck in the snows of a cruel Afghani winter—the Taliban government collapsed faster than even the U.S. military planners had expected.

What's the "takeaway" from this sequence of events? For one thing, the U.S. military was well prepared for its mission. Second, President Bush had surrounded himself with a superb team of national security professionals, all of whom contributed to the decision-making process that led to the war on terrorism. Those tasked by Bush with coalition-building—primarily Powell and to a lesser extent Cheney and Rumsfeld—did their job expertly. And finally, those responsible for bringing along the U.S. public, especially Rumsfeld, also performed beyond expectations.

Rumsfeld certainly played a unique role in advising President Bush and helping him to shape his thinking on the topic of defense (there will be much more on this in Chapter 12). Rumsfeld had been the most outspoken when it came to dealing directly and swiftly with "rogue" threats and to maintaining a strong and unambiguous national security policy. As mentioned in Chapter 8, he had had a discussion early in 2001 with President Bush in which he had emphasized the importance of changing the perception of America as a "risk-averse," "gun-shy" nation—and also of the importance of "leaning forward, not back" in the wake of a real or pending attack.

To some extent, therefore, he had plowed the ground onto which he and his colleagues—and his commander in chief—would later lead the nation.

THE RUMSFELD WAY

Mastering the agenda requires setting a direction: Rumsfeld feels that the essence of leadership comes down to putting an organization (or a country) on a particular path. Set a direction before making key operational decisions.

Define and build on core competencies: It sounds so fundamental, but companies to this day make the mistake of not properly defining their key business. Once the core business is defined, put the necessary resources behind it to make it grow.

To lead, embrace the difficult decisions: To fix the ailing Searle, Rumsfeld had to sell off twenty-three businesses and fire more than half of the corporate staff. Although these were difficult decisions, particularly for a family-run business, Rumsfeld knew that anything less would not turn the company around.

If you are committed to a topic (e.g., a strong national defense), never stop selling the message: One of the reasons

Rumsfeld excelled in the weeks following the terrorist attacks was his own level of preparedness. He had been speaking on the need for a strong and aggressive military for years and did not need a refresher course to fashion a response to the attacks.

THE PRAGMATIC LEADER

Making Results Count

When I took over [Searle]...I was asked to be
chief executive officer and run the company
in a manner that would be profitable, professional,
and consistent with the long term interests of
the shareholders, employees, customers....I was
asked to get results.

—DONALD RUMSFELD, SEPTEMBER 1979

I guess I'm kind of old-fashioned. I'm inclined to think that if you're going to cock it, you throw it, and you don't talk about it a lot. So my instinct is that what you do, you should go about your business and do what you think you have to do. I think anyone who thinks it's easy is wrong....And I don't think that people ought to judge outcomes until a sufficient time has passed to address what is clearly a very serious problem for the world.

—DONALD RUMSFELD, SEPTEMBER 2001

TO THIS POINT, we've spent a lot of time discussing Rumsfeld tactics, strategies, and vision: the ability to make things happen and anticipate future moves and counter-moves. Equally important, of course, is the ability to see things as they are.

And what do you do when the clearest possible picture of the present isn't clear enough? How do you avoid orga-nizational paralysis and—to use Rumsfeld's two-word mantra—"get results"?

Rumsfeld suggests that the answer lies in maintaining enough flexibility to deal with a variety of contingencies:

> *What we need to do is see if we can't get*
> *arranged in a way that we have the kind of flexibility*
> *to deal with a spectrum of—of contingencies and*
> *activities, rather than getting locked into a—a fixed*
> *set of something that seems probable today, which*
> *may very well not be probable at all.*

In other words, Rumsfeld is a *pragmatist*: someone who strikes a balance between solving short-term problems opportunistically and looking to the future to anticipate the contingencies. A pragmatist is also someone who real-izes that not all problems have solutions. Rumsfeld has quoted Israeli leader Shimon Peres to this effect:

If a problem has no solution, it may not
be a problem but a fact, not to be solved but
to be coped with over time.

The pragmatist strikes a balance. He or she throws enormous energy into solving a knotty and pressing problem—because to do less would be a waste of time and resources. And at the same time, he or she looks for evidence that the point of diminishing returns is being reached—and then backs off, as needed.

When Rumsfeld took over the Pentagon for the second time, early in 2001, he threw himself into the task of problem solving. In fact, he was roundly criticized as coming into the Defense Department like a bull in a china shop, attempting to effect massive change without mastering the new rules of Washington politics. He was perceived by many in the military as an out-of-step autocrat, who cared little about building effective alliances with key constituencies. (To be fair, his key detractors were the ones most interested in eschewing change and protecting the status quo.)

As noted in earlier chapters, Rumsfeld surely has his autocratic ways. But there was, and is, another side to the story. He perceived a true threat to America, although its precise outlines were as yet unclear. Rumsfeld's practical side instilled in him a sense of urgency, which compelled him to "stir the pot"—get people to break out of their molds and their established ways of thinking. No, they weren't going to change overnight. But neither would they be allowed to remain entrenched in the past:

It's been a process of trying to, not change things for
the sake of changing things, but to get a sense of
what's coming down the track on the freight train.

*And trying to figure out a way in which you can
affect that without waiting two years.*

Striking the balance—between motivating people and
demoralizing them by demanding too much too soon—is a
critical component of leadership. So is acting under conditions of uncertainty. Both are elements of *pragmatic leadership*—and Rumsfeld has a lot to tell us on this subject.

Management expert Peter Drucker has explored the
topic of change and uncertainty and has posed a clarifying
question for "strategic decision makers." Managers cannot
know what the future will bring. The key, therefore, lies in
developing an organization and a framework for dealing
with the unknowns of the future:

*The question that faces the strategic decision maker
is not 'what his organization should do tomorrow.'
It is, 'What do we have to do today to be ready
for an uncertain tomorrow?*

For years, Rumsfeld the pragmatist has been urging
America's leaders to take a harder line on those countries
that he felt posed the greatest risk to America's national
security (e.g., Iraq). And well before that, he had gotten
into the habit of taking controversial positions that often
involved "next-generation" scenarios (e.g., recommending
a missile shield to protect the United States from future
threats). It is not surprising, therefore, that he has ignited
controversy even as he has gained status and power.

THE PRAGMATIC BUSINESSMAN

In his writings, Rumsfeld warns managers not to make
"hockey-stick plans." This is what he calls plans and fore-

casts that project that key indicators—profits, revenue, or whatever—will fall for a year or two and then rise in future years. (Picture the shape of a hockey stick or a check mark.) He felt this was an unrealistic way to view business and warned that it often becomes a seductive and dangerous pattern: Managers get comfortable with the hockey stick, and wait year after year for things to turn around. The result? An enormous organizational weakness, and vulnerability.

Huge organizations (and none is larger than the U.S. military) cannot, and do not, turn on a dime. When Rumsfeld came to Searle, he insisted on a five-year contract. That's how long he figured it would take to turn the company around. He claimed subsequently that he didn't really need a contract but wanted one mainly "to signify the degree of commitment on my part."

Perhaps—but he surely wanted a guarantee of enough time to prove himself. And although he had ample confidence to make the move from the public to the private sector, he did not necessarily assume that the skills he had learned in government would translate immediately into the business arena. He suspected that the tactics he had employed at the Pentagon would have to be tempered to succeed in the business world. Here he is speaking to the editors at *Fortune* in 1979:

> *You might ask, do you get so bureaucratized*
> *that you forget how to operate any other way?*
> *No, it's a lot easier to decompress and not deal*
> *with a layer or two than add one or two. But it's not*
> *clear to me that skills are readily transferable*
> *between government and business...there's no*
> *particular reason why a successful businessman*
> *should be successful in government.*

An irony of history: Almost exactly twenty-two years later, *Newsweek* ran a story making exactly the same point and using Rumsfeld as its poster boy (the same story described in Chapter 2). Entitled "The Myth of the Super-CEO," the article purported to explain why Rumsfeld (for example) was having so much difficulty returning to Beltway politics, where power and structure work differently. "The record of senior businessmen in government is one of almost unrelieved disappointment," declared the magazine, only days before the September 11th tragedy.

Rumsfeld's early moves at Searle point to his ability to see things for what they are. Yes, he had a long-range vision for the company: more creative, more competitive, more energetic. But he also understood *today*, and acted on that understanding: divesting losing businesses, getting expenses in line by downsizing corporate staff, restructuring, focusing on the core business, and so on. In other words, he embodied Drucker's prescription: a highly practical manager who was able to simultaneously assess the current state of the business and prepare for the "uncertain tomorrow."

Rumsfeld was not naïve. He knew that his company's success would depend on his ability to set the right course—and, just as important, on his employees' ability to understand, buy into, and effectively execute the key imperatives. He "only had two hands," he said, and in order to be an effective leader, he needed to delegate. He said early on that things would not just happen "by command" (as in the Pentagon). One of the keys to success, therefore, would be to ensure that employees understood *why* the company was moving in a certain direction: "To a great extent success will depend on... execution," he once declared.

KNOW WHEN TO FOLD

Even as he went off to Searle in 1977, Rumsfeld knew he would someday return to the public sector. (In fact, his five-year contract at Searle, which Rumsfeld downplayed, may have been a tactic—prompted either by himself or by Searle—to pin him down and protect the company's interests.) And many of those who kept their eye on Rumsfeld also suspected that he had not abandoned his political ambitions. Nevertheless, most politicians and pundits were caught off guard when—in 1986—he announced his decision to run for president of the United States.

Over the years, Rumsfeld's self-serving political maneuverings had prompted the occasional question about his ultimate goal: Was he aiming for the presidency? When asked the question directly, Rumsfeld tended to either deflect the question or answer with what was probably the truth at the time: "I just don't know." That changed in the spring of 1986. In May, the *Wall Street Journal* ran a story with the following bold headline:

"Rumsfeld, With a Resume to Rival That of Bush, Prepares to Seek GOP Nomination for President."

Ronald Reagan was in his final two years of office, and his vice president—and logical successor—was the more experienced and palatable candidate George Herbert Walker Bush. The article stated that while Rumsfeld had not yet made any formal announcement of his intentions, friends of the political-operative-turned-successful-CEO said he was "deadly serious about the challenge":

Brimming with self-confidence, Mr. Rumsfeld is a man who relishes a challenge and fancies himself a pretty good practitioner of risk analysis....He has

concluded that there isn't much to lose in a
presidential race and plenty to gain.

According to the article, Rumsfeld understood that the front-runners for the 1988 campaign were George H. W. Bush and Jack Kemp, a former football star who then held a seat in the House of Representatives and was a darling of the conservative right (as it turned out, Kemp fizzled quickly, and Senator Bob Dole, who had won the Iowa caucus, became the key competitor). Rumsfeld was convinced that Bush and Kemp were not "as strong as many believed." Quoted in the piece were political analysts who felt that Rumsfeld was, in fact, well positioned to win ("perfectly positioned for the newly constituted GOP" was how one political consultant put it). The *Journal* also concluded that his "mainstream Republicanism" would serve him well.

The article also cited what the writer deemed his "political toughness" by retelling an episode that took place after the 1972 Nixon victory. Evidently, President Nixon's chief of staff, H. R. Haldeman, "had demanded the resignations of all top officials as a ploy to ease some out while avoiding the messy task of firing them." Rumsfeld, at the time head of the economic stabilization program, resisted, arguing that Haldeman's edict shouldn't apply to economic policy officials. "He got away with it," declared Representative Dick Cheney in 1986.

Henry Kissinger, too, thought that Rumsfeld might have what it takes to be president. (This is notable mainly because Kissinger so often crossed swords with Rumsfeld in their time together in the Ford administration.) In his 1999 memoir, he explained:

I came to believe that if he ever reached the
presidency, he might be a more comfortable chief

*executive than Cabinet colleague—indeed, he had the
makings of a strong President.*

But the Rumsfeld presidency was not to be. In a barely
noticeable story, the *Journal* ran a far different piece in
May of 1987:

"Rumsfeld Decides Against Seeking GOP Nomination."

In his memo to supporters, Rumsfeld explained his decision was based on a purely practical reason—lack of
money:

*For a dark horse, the improbable balance of
revenues and expenses early in the campaign raises
the specter of a deficit of several million dollars.
Deficit spending plagues this country. As a matter
of principle, I will not run on a deficit.*

And so, a year before the heavy work of the campaign
was to begin, here was Rumsfeld pulling out allegedly
because of a lack of money and a related "matter of principle." The ever-practical Rumsfeld knew he did not have
the war chest to mount a legitimate threat. Buy why not?
Is it possible that Rumsfeld, who may have lacked the
charisma and demeanor so essential to winning voters in a
presidential election, was simply not popular enough to
raise sufficient funds? And was an inadequate war chest the
real reason for his decision to pull out of the race?
Henry Kissinger, who said that "he regretted when he
[Rumsfeld] withdrew from elective office," put forth an
interesting psychological theory. True, Kissinger wrote that
the conditions were not "propitious," and this might have
been enough to scare off Rumsfeld. But there was another

possibility. Had Rumsfeld—whom Kissinger characterized as possessing "brilliant single-mindedness"—pulled away at the last minute because the prospect of failure proved too much for him? Or, as Kissinger phrased it artfully, "Had the reason for his tenacious procrastination all along been a congenital dread of a setback which made him recoil before the last hurdle because he could not bear the idea of failure?"

Perhaps. Far more likely, though, Rumsfeld figured that he simply could not win—that George Bush was too strong a candidate. After all, Reagan was America's most popular president since FDR, and Bush had been his vice president for eight years. Those would be very difficult circumstances to overcome. It seems likely that the Pragmatic Rumsfeld took precedence over the Ambitious Rumsfeld and decided against a race that was likely to end in an embarrassing defeat.

PRAGMATIC IN BATTLE

Since becoming a "secretary of war" (not an official title, but an appropriate one given his new role) on September 11th, Rumsfeld has been consistently realistic in his assessments and his approach to the war—and has demanded the same kind of realism from others. *The Economist* declared this about Rumsfeld:

> *A man with a job like his needs two*
> *connected qualities: an ability to inspire confidence,*
> *and the capacity to focus on the task at hand*
> *without getting bogged down in distractions.*
> *Mr. Rumsfeld has met both tests.*

Inspiring confidence and not getting bogged down: Both qualities have helped the secretary of defense to maintain a clear perspective and to manage the war effectively and efficiently. In briefings and interviews, he demonstrates his command of the small detail but also keeps the big picture in front of us. For example, in an interview with Bob Woodward discussing the days following the attacks, Rumsfeld had explained "that the first 36 hours of the crisis—the meetings and debates—were crucial. You cannot micromanage something like this. You've got to think of concepts and strategic direction." Again, we see the interplay between tomorrow's vision and today's execution.

On occasion he might lend some optimism to the situation—but he never lets his ego convince himself that things are going better than they really are. For example, in December of 2001, following the defeat of Taliban forces in several key Afghanistan provinces, one member of the Bush team was quoted as saying that the Taliban had been "defeated." Rumsfeld, eager to lower expectations, warned that there were still areas of resistance and that it would be premature to declare victory.

DEAL WITH DISAPPOINTMENTS
IN THE MIDST OF VICTORIES

In his December 2001 year-end review of the Defense Department, Rumsfeld once again showed his reluctance to paint an overly optimistic picture of the state of affairs of the military. In the following excerpts, he not only shows that he is realistic about the challenges of war but also admits there is much left to do:

> *We also have a lot of work ahead of us—in the war on terrorism, to be sure, but also here at home....Even before September 11th, we had agreed on the approach that puts a new emphasis*

on homeland security and helps us to prepare
for the full range of asymmetrical threats while
balancing the risks to our people, which are so
central to the success of the department....

He also discusses the progress (or lack thereof) in the battle to bring about meaningful change at the Pentagon. And he brings in other issues critical to the military, such as missile defense (a favorite topic of Rumsfeld) and the "Nuclear Posture Review":

In each of these areas there has been important
progress. At the same time, there were some
disappointments. The confirmation progress was
unacceptably slow....The budget process is not
really working well....

He then talks about how bureaucracy is impeding his efforts to manage the Defense Department and spend the taxpayers' money "wisely." While all of this may sound routine to managers in a corporate setting, it is rare for a politician to deliver such plainspoken and candid facts about the progress of his department.

This is especially true when one considers the time-frame and the circumstances. Rumsfeld delivered this news at the end of December 2001. By this time, the Taliban had fallen and al Qaeda in Afghanistan had been crushed and/or scattered, and Rumsfeld would have been excused if he had spent some time dwelling on those successes. Yes, he wrote how proud he was of the men and women of the Armed Forces who had served America so effectively. But the main focus of his message was on those things that needed improvement. Perhaps, as a pragmatist, he felt that this moment in history—when people were more concerned than ever with national defense—was the most opportune time to put the challenges and disappointments back on the table. By doing so at that precise moment in time, he knew that he was holding the best cards to wage a war on the status quo.

In summary, Rumsfeld's pragmatic streak has served him well—and the organizations he has headed—in his four decades of service in the public and private sectors. He deals with a messy present while preparing for an uncertain future, by drawing on a rich reserve of reality and opportunism.

THE RUMSFELD WAY

It's execution and results that count: The pragmatic Rumsfeld knows that he will be judged on results. Whether you run a large company or a small business, ultimately there is no substitute for results.

Maintain flexibility: Organizations and individuals must be prepared for an "uncertain tomorrow" and "asymmetrical threats." Be ready for the unexpected, maintain the flexibility to take on all contingencies rather than getting locked into a vision that "seems probable today, [but] which may very well not be probable at all."

Avoid false forecasts: Beware of the unrealistic forecast or plan. Rumsfeld warns against developing a "hockey-stick" mentality: forecasting one down year to be succeeded by a happy string of up years. Be realistic, and plan realistically.

Know when to cut your losses: Know when you don't have the money or when your opponent holds all the good cards. Don't run for president if you don't have a good shot at it. Live to fight (and serve) another day.

Deal with disappointments in the midst of victories: Celebrate victories, but also use them as an opportunity to fix what's still not right. Sometimes when the people around you are celebrating, they'll listen to your analysis of what's still broken.

THE DETERMINED WARRIOR

The War's Not Over until the Last Battle

You must attack. The only way to deal with terrorists is to take it to them. And that must be done....a lot of people use the word revenge or retribution or anger as though what you're doing is getting mad and getting even, and that is not what you're doing....they have attacked our way of life. We're free people. And either we're going to be free or we're not going to be ourselves. And therefore, the only choice we have is to attack. That is to say, to defend ourselves by taking the effort to do that.

—DONALD RUMSFELD, OCTOBER 2001

What do we mean by victory? Victory means liquidating the terrorist networks and putting them out of business. Victory means crippling the ability of terrorist organizations, and the states that sponsor them, to coerce our nation, intimidate our people, and disrupt our way of life. Victory means ensuring that Americans can continue to live as a free people.

—DONALD RUMSFELD, ADDRESS TO

THE MEN AND WOMEN OF

WHITEMAN AIR FORCE BASE, OCTOBER 19, 2001

WINSTON CHURCHILL ONCE DECREED: "In war: resolution. In defeat: defiance. In victory: magnanimity. In peace: goodwill." This final chapter begins with several Rumsfeld thoughts on the subject of victory and a Churchill quote because collectively, they reveal an intriguing aspect of the mindset of what I'll call the "Determined Warrior."

War often involves a complex amalgam of passion, calculation, and politics. Nations often go to war because their vital interests are threatened—a conclusion that is reached both in the mind and in the gut. Nations *win* at war when they keep emotion and calculation in fine balance. They devise effective strategies and implement those strategies as if their very lives depended on it—which in fact they may.

The Determined Warrior understands all this. He appeals to the emotions of his countrymen, but he also demands that they make the same kinds of calculations that he is making: What's possible? What's within our grasp? He makes the passionate speeches, but he also plods, and *persists*.

At the end of the day, this is one of the most interesting facets of Donald Rumsfeld: He persists. And not just as someone keeping a fertile brain occupied or amassing wealth and influence—he persists as a Determined Warrior, in service to a cause.

What explains Rumsfeld's determination and his durability? How has he been able to make move after move, infuriate powerful adversaries, and burn bridges—and still thrive? Some critics have pointed to what they see as Rumsfeld's naked, overweening ambition—an ambition without any philosophical grounding—as the key.

The *New Republic* once characterized him as having a "lack of ideological firmness" (they called him "George Bush [senior] without the thank-you notes"), and the extreme right-wing politico Pat Buchanan labeled Rumsfeld a "party pragmatist" with "no settled political philosophy." That accusation—of having no core convictions—has dogged Rumsfeld throughout his career and became common currency during his brief flirtation with the presidency in 1987.

But this Rumsfeld rebuke has little merit. One does not succeed in the most difficult of games without a steady flame burning somewhere toward the core. One doesn't achieve what he has without having a reservoir of conviction to draw upon. In Rumsfeld's case, that reservoir seems to consist of a profound commitment to the democratic principles of his country and of a society that generously presents both freedom and opportunity to its citizens. These are "old-fashioned" values, to be sure—but they more than suffice for Donald Rumsfeld.

And what happens when those convictions are challenged? The Determined Warrior comes out swinging. One of the interesting aspects of Rumsfeld's deeply held beliefs is that they are not restricted to the political arena. Rumsfeld the businessman also had deep convictions, and he wasn't afraid to act on them when they came under fire.

WHAT TO DO WHEN
BACKED INTO A CORNER

For an example, let's turn back the clock two decades, to when Rumsfeld encountered a thorny problem that threatened to inflict a mortal wound on his company. When he took over Searle in 1977, a compound called aspartame had been around the company for years. Its sweetness was accidentally discovered in 1965 by a junior Searle chemist, and in 1969, the firm initiated the FDA approval process with safety tests. Since patent protection lasts only seventeen years, the clock was ticking.

The regulatory process was exceedingly slow and cost the company millions of dollars. Finally, in 1974, the FDA approved the commercialization of aspartame. But the battle wasn't over. Following congressional hearings and an FDA examination of Searle's data keeping records (which turned up some inconsistencies), the FDA stayed its own approval in 1976.

In 1980, four years after the FDA's decision to block approval of aspartame, things were still bogged down in a seemingly impenetrable bureaucratic snare. That's when Rumsfeld—who had joined the company three years earlier—initiated a bold course of action that shocked everyone, including company insiders.

Searle had already written off more than $21 million of aspartame inventory that year, and things looked bleak. Searle executives felt that they had jumped through every hoop put before them by the FDA. Backed into a corner, Rumsfeld felt that the company had few choices. In October, against the advice of just about every attorney inside or outside the Beltway, the company sued the FDA, an unheard-of move for a pharmaceutical company whose future hinged on favorable rulings from that agency.

Much later, Rumsfeld talked about this watershed decision. Did he lash out in frustration against the government? No, he responded; it was not frustration that guided him. But the circumstances had combined in such a way as to make him "angry" and "energized," and this moved him to take the extraordinary step of suing the agency with which his company was supposed to work closely.

Within hours of the suit's being filed, an outside panel determined that aspartame did not pose the kind of health risks that some had feared. Following more studies and red tape, the FDA approved aspartame in July of 1981. The product, later branded as NutraSweet, went on to become a multibillion-dollar success story.

That short chapter speaks volumes about Rumsfeld's determination and tenacity. He was *angry*—truly angry— with the bureaucrats who he believed were unnecessarily harming his company. And he was *energized* by that anger, which he quickly turned to action, based upon a careful calculation of the risks and benefits of taking on one's own regulators. Ultimately, he prevailed. By 1984, NutraSweet was a $400-million product and was responsible for half the company's operating income.

In 1985, more than eight years after Rumsfeld arrived at Searle, he helped facilitate the sale of the (now healthy) company to Monsanto. That sale netted Rumsfeld some $12 million, making him one of the richest former congressmen in U.S. history.

Then, in 1990, Rumsfeld took the reins of electronics giant General Instrument Corporation, a company specializing in communications and broadband technology. When that firm was sold to Motorola in 1993, Rumsfeld's fortunes were increased by several more million dollars.

In 2001, *Forbes* tried to put a number on Rumsfeld's fortune. Using financial disclosure forms that he provided, they estimated his net worth at between $55 and $214 million. Approximately 40 percent of the total was estimated to consist of limited partnerships and other private investments.

These numbers are pertinent mainly because they demonstrate that Rumsfeld was certainly in a position to retire to his vacation home in New Mexico and work on his squash game. Instead, in January of 2001, he returned to the frenzied life of public service as Pentagon CEO. Yes, one can point to the addictive qualities of working in the halls of power. But surely there is something else going on here—a sense of commitment, and purpose, that places a multimillionaire past retirement age back into the crosshairs of public service.

CONSUMED BY A CAUSE

One arena in which Rumsfeld the Determined Warrior shows up most regularly is the realm of missile defense, which has consumed his agenda for years. He has spoken extensively on the topic, usually in the context of "threats from rogue states or nations." Despite determined opposition from policy makers and pundits—who claim that missile defense is both unnecessary and unworkable—he has held his ground on this issue and seldom has missed an opportunity to spread his missile-defense gospel.

In 1996, Rumsfeld was convinced to assist in the management of Bob Dole's futile presidential campaign against incumbent Bill Clinton. Dole was trounced, but before going down, he did manage to score some points by incorporating several of Rumsfeld's hawkish themes into his fledgling campaign. He attacked Clinton on his stance toward Iraq and recommended that the United States develop a national missile shield by 2003. These ideas would be echoed four years later by Governor George Bush in his own run for the White House. Noted military policy expert Michael T. Klare, writing in *The Nation* in January 2001, declared that, "Governor Bush articulated other themes originally crafted by Rumsfeld during the Dole campaign of 1996."

In May of 2000, presidential candidate Bush gave an important speech on reducing nuclear arms and "building effective missile defense...at the earliest possible date." When delivering this speech, Bush surrounded himself (literally) with five prominent individuals who he said aided him in formulating his defense plans. The five standing at his side were Henry Kissinger, George Schultz, Brent Scowcroft, Colin Powell, and Donald Rumsfeld.

Two years earlier, Rumsfeld was asked to chair the Commission to Assess the Ballistic Missile Threat to the United States. A blue ribbon panel chartered by Congress, its goal was to calculate how much time hostile countries such as Iran and North Korea would need before they would be able to launch missiles that could hit the United States.

In order to complete their task, Rumsfeld, adamant that he not be stonewalled, first had to convince reluctant CIA director George Tenet to give the commission access to classified intelligence information. According to longtime *Washington Post* reporter Bradley Graham, author of the book *Hit to Kill*, the commission represented a major turning point in the debate over missile defense:

If there was ever a single moment in the late 1990s when events began to turn in favor of those advocating a national missile defense, this was it. The meeting with Tenet opened the way for Rumsfeld and his commission to conduct a searing reassessment of the ballistic missile threat to the United States.

The commission ultimately issued a unanimous report that claimed that certain hostile regimes could have missiles that could hit the United States within five years (ten years for Iraq), far sooner than the existing intelligence reports indicated. U.S. intelligence estimated that these countries would require fifteen years to reach that level of missile capability. As a result, the commission recommended a reassessment of American intelligence gathering policy, as well as the creation of a national missile defense (NMD) system. These controversial findings explained why the Rumsfeld commission's report attracted so much attention and placed Rumsfeld at the epicenter of the national missile shield debate.

While some government officials and experts dismissed the commission's findings as simplistic or hyperbolic, the commission's report impressed many inside the Beltway (but infuriated the intelligence community for obvious reasons). Bradley Graham offers an explanation for why the report was taken so seriously: "By speaking in a unanimous voice, the commissioners received a serious hearing in a national debate...While earlier attempts at assessing the threat, including the government's own effort, had been discounted as politically tinged, the Rumsfeld group's effort emerged as perhaps the single most authoritative view."

Rumsfeld views NMD as an essential ingredient in a larger transformation of the American military—and, by extension, a more effective defense of this country. His larger goal is to create more mobile forces capable of protecting the United States from hostile countries that he believes are gaining greater capabilities, specifically through the development of weapons of mass destruction.

In the speech on "Strategic Imperatives" delivered in 1998, Rumsfeld spoke on the complexity of American foreign policy and the need for setting the right priorities:

"There is not likely to be any single, simple 'doctrine' to guide us. It is going to take judgment, common sense, and the wisdom to set the right priorities—and the courage and perseverance to lead."

In late 2001, Rumsfeld summarized his thoughts on why he felt it was time for a new model for the military and why a "simple doctrine" would not be sufficient to guide military policy in the future. While he made this statement after September 11th, Rumsfeld's thinking on the subject had not changed in years:

We need to recognize that it's unlikely that armies, navies and airforces are going to attack us because we have such strong forces. Therefore, the asymmetrical threats—ballistic missiles, cruise missiles, terrorist attacks, cyber-attacks—are ways they can leverage their capabilities.

In Rumsfeld's view of the world, we must abandon the Cold War paradigm and shift away from a "threats-based" military to a "capabilities-based" military, one flexible enough to deal with the aforementioned asymmetrical threats.

MAKING ENEMIES WITH MISSILE DEFENSE

Many of Rumsfeld's opinions have won him detractors over the years. But of all Rumsfeld's views, it is his seemingly intractable position on missile defense (and similar next-generation defense plans) that have elicited the most controversy. Senate Majority Leader Tom Daschle and Foreign Relations Committee Chairman Joe Biden (among many others) have made their views widely known, strongly opposing the funding of missile defense.

Rumsfeld's critics do not end at U.S. borders. In the spring of 2001, the European edition of the *Wall Street Journal* ran a highly critical, politically charged story entitled "Europe, Meet Mr. Rumsfeld." The writer, Jeffrey Gedmin, declared that "Rumsfeld appears to hold special honors when it comes to fueling European anxieties." The lengthy piece articulated many of Europeans' apprehensions with Rumsfeld's extreme views, calling him "a high-tech dreamer and a missile defense ideologue." The article also said of Rumsfeld that his "ruthless pragmatism and complete lack of sentimentality are...hard to swallow."

The U.S. press has criticized Rumsfeld on this issue as well. Just two days before the September 11th attacks, for example, CNN's Wolf Blitzer asked the defense secretary why America should "spend these billions and billions of dollars for a missile defense system that may or may not work." Rumsfeld's response was unequivocal:

There have been people making those kinds of arguments since the beginning of this country. Why should we waste money learning how to fly? Why did the Wright brothers try to learn how to fly airplanes? They'll never do it. Why do we ever have the Corona program [the first overhead satellite system]...? It'll never work. Eleven straight failures, and now it's one of the most important aspects of our intelligence-gathering capability.

It is worth pointing out that Rumsfeld's views on NMD have been echoed, at one time or another, by at least three other key members of the Bush team: Colin Powell, Condoleezza Rice, and Dick Cheney. At least prior to the events of September 11th—when so many priorities shifted abruptly—all were in agreement that the deployment of some sort of missile defense should be a national priority. Still, no one has argued more passionately for NMD than Rumsfeld, and he has stuck to his high-tech guns despite vociferous and skilled opposition. Again, we see evidence of the Determined Warrior, who wins in part by persistence.

A SPACE PEARL HARBOR

The 1998 Rumsfeld commission may have made headlines, but it was another, less high-profile commission that revealed an even more extreme side of Donald Rumsfeld. That commission, also headed by Rumsfeld, released its findings in January 2001, the same day that Rumsfeld was describing "a twenty-first-century military" to the Senate Armed Forces Committee during his confirmation hearings. Known officially as the Commission to Assess United States National Security Space Management and Organization, it was soon dubbed the "Space Commission."

Its findings included a disturbing warning for America. Here is the way Michael Krepon summed it up in a lengthy article entitled "Lost in Space" that appeared in *Foreign Affairs*:

> *The study warns that the United States may someday soon face a "Space Pearl Harbor"—that is, a devastating sneak attack against U.S. satellites orbiting the planet....Space warfare, the commission argues, has become a 'virtual certainty.'*

The panelists' reasoning seemed logical enough. As Rumsfeld put it in the commission's report, history reveals that "every medium—air, land, and sea—has seen conflict. Reality indicates that space will be no different."

But Rumsfeld's reasoning failed to impress many experts. Krepon, who is president emeritus of the Henry L.

Stimson Center, felt that the recommendations of the commission, which argued for the weaponization of space, were misguided. Krepon argued that "the best way to protect space commerce and U.S. national security...is to avoid ASAT'S [antisatellite weapons] and weapons in space in the first place."

Other authorities also weighed in on Rumsfeld's ideas on weaponizing space. In an opinion piece in the *Chicago Tribune*, Michael E. O'Hanlon, Senior Fellow of Foreign Policy Studies at the Brookings Institution, urged Rumsfeld to "stay out of the heavens," claiming that pursuing such a course of action was "premature." Proclaimed O'Hanlon: "The United States should not race against itself." Such a move, O'Hanlon argued, would simply provoke China and Russia into developing similar technologies, which would not be in America's best interest.

THE SPOILS OF PERSEVERANCE

What happens when a Determined Warrior takes unpopular positions? First, he generates opposition, even enemies—which at Rumsfeld's stage of life may not be a consequential consideration. Second, he generates debate, which Rumsfeld surely welcomes. (There will be no NMD without a spirited debate of its pros and cons.) And finally—and perhaps incidentally—he generates opportunities.

Rumsfeld's hawkish advocacy of a strong military featuring missile and other star wars–like defense weapons may have won him his job as secretary of defense in the Bush administration. Of all the candidates on Bush's short list to head the Pentagon, Rumsfeld was one of the most vocal advocates for ballistic missile defense and for a tougher stance toward Russia and China.

The other factor that probably *ensured* his appointment was Vice President Dick Cheney. Three decades earlier, the Rumsfeld/Cheney team had dominated the Ford White House. Cheney, who was Rumsfeld's protégé back then, was not only indebted to Rumsfeld (he became Rumsfeld's successor as chief of staff when Rumsfeld became defense secretary), he also knew him to be a formidable asset, even in his later years. As Cheney put it, candidly, "I never bought the criticism that somehow he was a relic of the past." The reuniting of the two, some pundits felt, was a re-creation of the Ford administration, in which two strong-willed, experienced politicos would be able to steer things their own way with a less experienced president in the Oval Office.

Bush's decision to appoint Rumsfeld surprised many, but perhaps not those closest to the situation. While Rumsfeld was not Bush's first (and perhaps not even second) choice as secretary of defense, the Rumsfeld selection certainly confirmed Bush's commitment to a national antimissile system. Bush had several prominent advisers on the subject of national security and missile defense, chief among them Condoleezza Rice, who had begun counseling him after Bush's father introduced the two at the family's summer home in Kennebunkport in 1998.

However, Bush recalled a briefing that made a difference in formulating his thoughts on the subject of missile defense. That meeting took place with Donald Rumsfeld in May of 1999. In it, Rumsfeld discussed the issues of global threats and missile defense. According to author Bradley Graham, Bush later declared that the briefing "made eminent sense; it kind of confirmed my philosophy."

Henry Kissinger is confident that Donald Rumsfeld has had a significant impact on George W. Bush's thinking on missile defense: "There is absolutely no doubt that Rumsfeld made an absolutely seminal contribution to the thinking of this country, and, I am sure, of the candidate, on missile defense." (As noted in May of 2000, candidate Bush met privately for a briefing with five prominent individuals, including Kissinger and Rumsfeld.)

As noted earlier, Bush adopted several Rumsfeld themes in his own campaigns and speeches. In two talks that he gave at the Citadel (the first in 1999), Bush made it known that he "fully endorsed" Rumsfeld's plan to transform the military. That's when Bush spoke of a new vision for the military and of how a "rallying point of a defining mission is needed."

With the President's backing, Rumsfeld's plan soon began to take shape. Emboldened by both the September 11th tragedy and the mandate of the commander in chief, the Department of Defense announced "the redesignation of the Ballistic Missile Defense Organization (BMDO) as the Missile Defense Agency" in early 2002. After years of rhetoric and commissions, the BMDO was elevated to agency status, giving it more authority and funding. It had been four years since Rumsfeld had issued his report on ballistic missile threats, and it was that report that had helped to ignite the GOP's push for a national missile shield.

What larger lessons can we glean from Rumsfeld's approach to missile defense? Once again, we see the Determined Warrior at work. He draws on a reservoir of commitment and uses both his gut and his intellect to advance the cause. He is persistent in his values, but he is opportunistic in the realization of those values. (NMD is not an end in itself; it is merely the current best way—in Rumsfeld's opinion—to get to a longstanding larger goal.) And while controversial ideas beget enemies, they also make new friends and create new opportunities. And finally, those opportunities themselves are not opportunities for self-aggrandizement—they are opportunities to do battle, once again, for the cause.

THE RUMSFELD WAY

Never underestimate the importance of determination: Rumsfeld's perseverance has played an important role throughout his four-decade career. The ability to stick with something, particularly in the face of criticism, is a trait that may spell the difference between success and failure.

Do not be afraid to champion your cause in a public forum: Even though Rumsfeld's favorite topic (NMD) incited analysts and policy makers alike, he never bowed to pressure or compromised his position. His close association with that topic may have played a major factor in his winning the position of defense secretary in 2001.

Don't get angry, get energized: In the midst of a critical battle against a government agency's bureaucracy, Rumsfeld said that he did not get frustrated or angry, he got energized. Draw on conviction to feel anger, and draw on that anger to shape a plan that comes from the head as well as the heart.

View opposition as an opportunity, not a threat: Opposition to Rumsfeld's ideas on missile defense did not derail him. Instead, it gave him a larger platform to express his views and may have helped win him his post in the Bush administration (the only defense secretary to hold the office twice). Had he been put off by his critics and foes, the "Rumsfeld as leader" story may never have been written.

THE "AXIS OF EVIL"

Concerted efforts by a number of overtly or potentially hostile nations to acquire ballistic missiles with biological or nuclear payloads pose a growing threat to the United States, its deployed forces, its friends and allies. These newer, developing threats in North Korea, Iran and Iraq are in addition to those still posed by the existing missile arsenals of Russia and China....Under some plausible scenarios...the U.S. might have little or no warning before operational deployment.

—FROM THE REPORT TO ASSESS THE BALLISTIC MISSILE THREAT TO THE UNITED STATES (THE "RUMSFELD REPORT," JULY 1998)

Our...goal is to prevent regimes that sponsor terror from threatening America or our friends and allies with weapons of mass destruction. Some of these regimes have been pretty quiet since Sept. 11th. But we know their true nature. North Korea is a regime arming with missiles and weapons of mass destruction....Iran aggressively pursues these weapons and exports terror....Iraq continues to flaunt its hostility towards America and to support terror....States like these and their terrorist allies constitute an axis of evil....

—PRESIDENT GEORGE W. BUSH,

IN HIS FIRST STATE OF THE UNION ADDRESS,

JANUARY 29, 2002

IN THE EARLY PART OF 2002, as this book went to press, President Bush was pushing for an additional $48 billion in defense spending for 2003 and for a $120 billion increase by 2007—a military buildup not seen since the Reagan days. This increase would mean that the Pentagon budget would skyrocket to $451 billion by 2007. Given the widespread support for the war against terrorism, as well as the president's soaring approval rating (over 80%), the plan is likely to win bipartisan support. "The president will get largely what he asks for in this area," declared Democratic Senator Kent Conrad, who chairs the Senate Budget Committee, to the *New York Times*. "We're at war, and when the president asks for additional resources for national defense, he generally gets it."

THE NEW "AXIS OF EVIL"

In his first State of the Union address in early 2002, President Bush outlined his vision for the future of the U.S. battle against terrorism. Bush's rhetoric evoked the tone and language of another popular wartime president, Franklin Delano Roosevelt. In the days that followed, it was Bush's designation of three countries that kept Beltway tongues wagging. In his address, he singled out Iraq, Iran, and North Korea as "an axis of evil," conjuring up images of the World War II Axis powers of Germany, Japan, and Italy.

To some, it sounded like nothing less than a declaration of war on the regimes of those three countries. As a result, many were stunned by Bush's boldness in singling out and isolating three nations as an "axis." (Iran and Iraq, for example, had killed a million troops in their war against *each other*, hardly making those two an "axis.") In addition, Iran had played a minor role in toppling the Taliban in Afghanistan, and there were many other states Bush could have named (e.g., Libya, Syria). Within days, irate statements were issued from officials of the aforementioned countries.

For example, Ayatollah Ali Khamenei, the supreme religious leader of Iran, issued an angry retort, claiming that Bush sounded like a man who has a "thirst for human blood." There was also a backlash in the streets of Iran, when millions turned out to protest the Bush pronouncements during their Islamic revolution anniversary march (Iranian protestors burned the American flag, the first time that had happened there in years). And it wasn't only the named "axis countries" that were up in arms.

Within days, it also became apparent that several European allies were more than a little disturbed by Bush's speech. For example, Joschka Fischer, Germany's foreign minister, was not the sole European voice when he criticized the United States for treating "its allies like satellite states" and warning the U.S. against moving "unilaterally against such countries as Iraq." He added another sentiment that was likely shared by many other foreign leaders when he asserted: "A world with six billion people will not be led into a peaceful future by the mightiest power alone."

Bush's harsh oratory in his address suggested to some that the administration assumed the post–September 11th geopolitical calculus had shifted dramatically, giving the

United States the moral high ground to deal with these dangerous regimes.

PRESCIENCE OR ANCIENT HISTORY?

Although a four-year-old report may be considered ancient history in the fast moving intelligence world, the three "axis of evil" countries were singled out in Rumsfeld's 1998 Report (on assessing ballistic missile threats). In the section entitled "Countries with Scud-Based Missile Infrastructures," the three were precisely (and exclusively, at least in the unclassified version of the report) listed as the countries that posed a "substantial" danger to the U.S.:

> *The extraordinary level of resources North Korea and Iran are now devoting to developing their own ballistic missile capabilities poses a substantial and immediate danger to the U.S., its vital interests and its allies.*

In the month following the issuance of the Rumsfeld Report, North Korea launched a three-stage ballistic missile (bearing a satellite) that had traveled more than 1,600 kilometers (over the Pacific). This event gave credence to at least a portion of Rumsfeld's findings. In January of 2001, the editorial page of the *Wall Street Journal* cited that fact, and weighed in on Rumsfeld's reports (both Rumsfeld I and Rumsfeld II).

The paper decreed that Rumsfeld's Commission was "the latest evidence of why he is precisely the Defense Secretary the nation needs at this point in history...." They also said that the second Rumsfeld Report (issued by the Space Commission) "is up there in importance with the report of the first Rumsfeld Commission." The editorial also took a jab at President Clinton in his final week in office: "Rumsfeld I put the lie to the Clinton Administration's blithe assertion that there is nothing to worry about."

Apparently, key members of the Bush administration thought that there was plenty to worry about and had felt that way for quite some time. In addition to the two commissions he chaired, Rumsfeld initiated other actions that revealed the depth of his commitment to protect American interests from hostile regimes. In 1998, for example, both Rumsfeld and his ultra-hawkish deputy, Paul Wolfowitz, had signed a letter from the Project for the New American Century (a conservative think tank) to President Clinton, asking for Saddam Hussein's removal from power in Iraq.

When Henry Kissinger was asked about his opinion of the impact of the first Rumsfeld Report on President Bush's first State of the Union address, he answered that he did not know the direct influence. However, he did add the following: "To the extent that the Rumsfeld Report is meaningful, it is because it is essentially true. These are three states that have a high capacity of producing weapons of mass destruction and that have shown enormous hostility to the environment in which they operate."

THE DETERMINED WARRIOR'S NEXT BATTLE

Two weeks after Bush's State of the Union address, the administration issued its harshest declaration on Iraq since the Gulf War. In the lead story in that day's paper, the *New York Times* headline declared [Colin] Powell says U.S. is Weighing Ways to Topple Hussein." The piece cited Bush's State of the Union address, and said that "the administration was considering a variety of options to topple Saddam Hussein." The fact that Secretary of State Powell delivered this message underscored the seriousness of the situation, since Powell is known to be the least hawkish of Bush's closest advisers.

Perhaps more important, however, was the speed with which events were unfolding. Fourteen days after the "axis of evil" speech came the Powell pronouncement warning of potential military action against the Iraqi leader. While Powell said that for years the U.S. had supported a "regime change" in Iraq, it appeared that the administration felt that the time had come to take decisive action against Baghdad. In the same State of the Union speech, Bush made it eminently clear that U.S. patience was running out. Here is the defiant Bush throwing down the gauntlet:

> *Time is not on our side. I will not wait on events as dangers gather. I will not stand by as peril draws closer and closer....America will not permit the world's most dangerous regimes to threaten us with the world's most destructive weapons. Our war on terror is well begun, but it is only begun. This campaign may not be finished on our watch, yet it must be and it will be waged on our watch.*

Sitting quietly in the front row, taking in every word, was a slight-looking man with circular spectacles, a strange squint, and a serious countenance. As the camera panned his way, he ignored it, apparently too deep in thought to notice such things. Absent the lectern and the microphone, he seemed somehow diminished, older than his 69 years and more than a little tired. However, a more discerning eye could see the Determined Warrior, plotting his next moves, fighting future battles, trying to think two steps ahead of those he knew were hell-bent on destroying the things he believed in so deeply.

ACKNOWLEDGMENTS

IN WRITING THIS BOOK, I was fortunate to secure the assistance of several experts whose guidance and insights made this a far richer work. For his numerous suggestions, I thank Dr. Richard J. Semiatin, Academic Director, American Politics Program and Assistant Professor of Political Science, American University.

I would also like to acknowledge and offer my gratitude to Dr. Henry Kissinger for his cooperation. Dr. Kissinger was kind enough to offer his insights on several pertinent topics related to this book, and I am grateful to him for clarifying several essential points. His views made a substantial contribution to helping me to bridge the gap between the Donald Rumsfeld of the Ford White House and the Donald Rumsfeld of today. He also shared his thoughts on the many challenges confronting the Bush administration and its current war on terrorism, and I am indebted to him for his articulate analysis.

I also acknowledge the stellar efforts of two individuals whom I have had the good fortune to work with on several projects throughout the years. To Dr. David Sicilia, business historian, professor and author, I offer my sincere appreciation for his numerous suggestions and contributions (including the Rumsfeld chronology that appears in Chapter 2). To author, editor, and friend, Jeffrey L. Cruikshank, who enriched this book from the moment he touched it, I offer my heartfelt appreciation. Jeff has many talents that are invaluable to authors, not the least of which is an unvarnished candor.

My gratitude to my wife, Nancy Krames, transcends the usual note of thanks that most author-husbands offer their wives in this portion of the book. Nancy played a key role in the research and editing phases of the project, and her analytical mind never stopped working. Her persistent questioning and probing (while sometimes exasperating), helped me to never lose sight of the big picture. On many important levels, I am blessed to have such a wonderful partner.

At McGraw-Hill, I am fortunate to be surrounded by a team of talented professionals who share my passion for publishing. For helping to bring this book to life, I send a special note of thanks to Michel Spitzer, whose idea it originally was to pursue a book on Donald Rumsfeld. Thanks also go to my editor and publisher, Philip Ruppel, and to Lydia Rinaldi, Lynda Luppino, and Tom Lau for a superb cover design. I also thank those in the marketing group who helped create the package for this book—especially Amanda Yee, Karen Brunetto, David Dell'accio, Anthony Sarchiapone, Dan Stivers, and Chitra Bopardikar and Allyson Arias for their efforts internationally. Also thanks to Donna Gauthier for always looking after my books, and to the entire Burr Ridge team for their support.

And for his publishing instincts and belief in this project from its inception, I offer my gratitude to Theodore Nardin.

A singular note of appreciation must go to one of the industry's finest production managers, Peter McCurdy. It is Peter who transformed the paragraphs and pages into the book you now hold, and did so with an abundance of patience under extraordinary circumstances. I also acknowledge the fine work of his collaborators, text designer José Fonfrias and Patty Wallenburg, owner of TypeWriting, our typesetter.

Lastly, for assistance in the developmental stages of the project, I thank Monica Eckman, D.T. of Buckeye Drive, and Dr. Henry Kaufman (a real mensch), for their roles in helping to coordinate the final, vital pieces of the project.

To my parents, Barton and Trudy (and Aunt Henny), I thank them for their sacrifices and their love (and for insisting on Bronx Science and a Selectric typewriter over the alternatives). Sedgewick Avenue is a long way from the Windy City, but the hard-fought lessons they instilled in me on that one city block continue to guide me to this day.

SOURCES AND NOTES

AS WAS MENTIONED in the introduction to this book, one of the most surprising aspects of researching Donald Rumsfeld was the lack of any definitive source on the subject. Absent any single book or memoir, the Rumsfeld body of knowledge that provided a foundation for this book emerged from more than 200 books, articles, speeches, reports, interviews, etc. One key source was *Political Profiles: The Nixon–Ford Years*, edited by Eleanora W. Schoenebaum (New York: Facts on File, 1979). This was the most complete profile/chronology of Donald Rumsfeld that was unearthed in the researching of this book.

Many of the secondary sources proved invaluable for providing historical facts, rich context, background, or anecdotes. When taken in their entirety, they allowed this author to paint what I hope will be an illuminating and compelling portrait while also providing the necessary context to draw something of a leadership blueprint that others might follow to achieve the type of success enjoyed by our subject.

One of the challenges of researching Rumsfeld is that his most defining acts essentially took place in two acts. Most of act I took place in the 1970s to the mid-1980s, when he made his mark in both government and industry. Although Rumsfeld didn't disappear entirely in between, act II began in 1998 and continues to the present day. While there were many sources that proved helpful, several of the works deserve to be singled out for their contribution to this work and their importance to this author.

For act I, it was one profile and several noteworthy biographies that proved the most helpful. Gerald Ford's *A Time to Heal* (New York: Harper & Row, 1979) was particularly helpful in providing the big picture surrounding the events of Watergate, the pardon of President Nixon, and Rumsfeld's rise to prominence in Ford's White House. However, other, more critical volumes were also necessary in order to dig deeper into the events of 1974–1976. Henry Kissinger's third (and final) volume of his memoirs, *Years of Renewal* (New York: Simon & Schuster, 1999), was an important book for gaining insights into the events surrounding the transition to the Ford White House and the key players inside the administration, including Rumsfeld.

Another key memoir for understanding the politics of the Ford administration was Robert Hartmann's *Palace Politics: An Inside Account of the Ford Years* (New York: McGraw-Hill, 1980). Of all of the memoirs, this was the only one to devote an entire chapter to Rumsfeld ("Rummy's Run"), and this material was invaluable in learning of Rumsfeld's machinations (which became the subject of so much speculation in the ensuing years).

Pulitzer Prize–winning journalist Clark Mollenhoff's work, *The Man Who Pardoned Nixon: A Documented Account of Gerald Ford's Presidential Retreat from Credibility* (New York: St. Martin's Press, 1976, published in association with The K. S. Giniger Company, Inc., New York), helped to validate much of the information regarding the inner workings of the Ford White House.

Other key sources included James Cannon's *Time and Chance* (New York: Harper-Collins, 1994), Ron Nessen's *It Sure Looks Different from the Inside* (Chicago: Playboy

Press, 1978), and William G. Hyland's *Mortal Rivals: Superpower Relations from Nixon to Reagan* (New York: Random House, 1987). Additional important sources for the Ford years included Bernard Firestone and Alexej Ugrinsky's *Gerald R. Ford and the Politics of Post-Watergate America* (Westport, Connecticut: Greenwood Press, 1993; two volumes), John Robert Greene's *The Presidency of Gerald R. Ford* (Lawrence, Kan.: University Press of Kansas, 1995) and John Osborne's *White House Watch: The Ford Years* (Washington, D.C.: New Republic Books, 1977).

I would also like to cite the excellent work of Bradley Graham of *The Washington Post* and his groundbreaking book, *Hit to Kill: The New Battle Over Shielding America from Missile Attack* (New York: Public Affairs, 2001). In addition to providing the most comprehensive coverage of the spirited debate over missile defense, the book was also invaluable in providing details (and a chronology) of Rumsfeld's first briefing of George W. Bush in 1999.

One important source for Rumsfeld as CEO of G. D. Searle was a book by Joseph McCann entitled *Sweet Success: How NutraSweet Created a Billion Dollar Business*, Homewood, Illinois: Business One Irwin, 1990 (for the record, I was the editor of that work). To the best of my knowledge, it was the only book ever published that detailed the business practices of Donald Rumsfeld and his turnaround of Searle; it proved to be particularly valuable in helping to tell the business side of the Rumsfeld story.

In addition to the books and the memoirs, several articles, many decades old, proved to be invaluable in completing the leadership style and practices of the subject. *Time* magazine's story entitled "Inside the War Room," which appeared in the January 29, 2002 issue, provided one of the most detailed accounts of the events and the decision making that took place in the Bush White House in the minutes, hours, and days following the September 11th attacks.

As the book was nearing completion, *Esquire* published a compelling account by Wil S. Hylton entitled "Dick & Don Go to War" in their February 2002 issue. This highly detailed account broke new ground on the events surrounding the Halloween Massacre of 1975, as well as providing background material on Rumsfeld's role in getting Gerald Ford to run and defeat Charles Halleck in the 1965 election for minority house leader.

Fortune magazine published several pieces that spanned more than two decades that helped complete the "Rumsfeld as CEO" picture. The "Ten Toughest Bosses" piece in 1980 revealed the darker, more volatile side of Rumsfeld's personality. "A Politician Turned Executive Surveys Both Worlds," published September 10, 1979, was the most complete piece on Rumsfeld's transition from government to business.

Finally, two of Rumsfeld's speeches were indispensable in helping to get beneath the surface and into what Mark Twain called "the clothes and buttons of a man" (which is how he described the essence of biography). The first was delivered to the Ethics & Public Policy Center in Washington, D.C., on November 20, 1985, and was entitled "Values Have Consequences." That speech provided the foundation for Chapter 5 of this book on values and the role they play in decision making and leading.

"Strategic Imperatives in East Asia," a speech given to the Heritage Foundation in March of 1998, was illuminating in that it foreshadowed the positions and ideals that Rumsfeld would bring to the Bush White House and the war against terrorism in 2001. It showed the hawkish nature of Rumsfeld and explained why an ambiguous foreign policy would be dangerous in that it would lead to "miscalculations" on the part of America's enemies, with possible dire consequences.

Rumsfeld's Return

The source for the story of Nixon's resignation and Ford's ride into Washington in which Ford wrote "Rumsfeld" as the car passed into Virginia was Bob Woodward and Carl Bernstein's *The Final Days* (New York: Simon & Schuster, 1976, pp. 451–452).
The Rumsfeld exchange with reporters came from a Department of Defense news briefing with Secretary Rumsfeld , January 11, 2002.

Chapter 1

"I think he is the one...." Dr. Henry Kissinger, interview with the author, February 19, 2002.
Rumsfeld's characterization as "Darth Vader" appeared in Jason Vest's article, "Darth Rumsfeld," *The American Prospect*, Princeton, February 26, 2001, Vol. 12, iss. 4, p. 20.
"Mr. Rumsfeld's waffle quotient...." "Old Hawk Learns New Tricks," *The Economist*, October 13, 2001, p. 58.
"Why should Ho Chi Minh believe me...." and Hugh Sidey, "Tortuous Road to Decision—and Lady Bird's Role," *Life*, April 12, 1968, p. 32.
"Successful politicians are insecure and intimidated men...." Hugh Sidey, "Not Enough Politics, Not Enough Partisanship," *Life*, November 15, 1968, p. 8.
"Great crises are marked by their memorable moments...." Donald Rumsfeld (who also quoted Winston Churchill), speech delivered in a Message to U.S. Forces, DOD Civilians, September 12, 2001, Department of Defense Website.

"We are all Watergate junkies…" was said by President Ford's army aide, Major Bob Barrett.

Chapter 2

"The strength that matters most is not the strength of arms.…" Official welcoming ceremony for Secretary of Defense Rumsfeld, January 26, 2001.

"The worst day of his tenure has proved to be the best for his professional fortunes.…" Susan Baer, *Playing by His Own Rules, Baltimore Sun*, December 9, 2001, p. 6e.

Schoenebaum, *Political Profiles*, 1979, pp. 551–554. Several pieces of vital information regarding the life of Donald Rumsfeld came from this rare profile, which was compiled shortly after his departure from government in 1976.

"A Rumsfeld Chronology" was compiled from two sources: the Department of Defense Website, http://www.defenselink.mil/bios/secdef_bio.html, and David B. Sicilia and Robert Sobel, eds., *Biographical Directory of the United States Executive Branch, 1774–2001* (Westport, Conn.: Greenwood, 2002).

"exuding a style suggestive of a conservative Kennedy." Schoenebaum, *Political Profiles*, 1979, p. 551.

"ought to be kept around if for no other reason…" ibid, p. 552.

The story of Gerald Ford unseating Charles W. Halleck appeared in Ford's *A Time to Heal*, 1979.

"The fact that he [Rumsfeld] was in the Nixon White House.…" Ibid.

The story of the "Halloween Massacre" was compiled from several sources. The key article was Wil S. Hylton, "Dick & Don Go to War" in *Esquire*, February 2002, pp. 80–89. This piece included George Herbert Walker Bush's telegram to President Ford, *"I do not have politics out of my system.…*

William G. Hyland. *Mortal Rivals: Superpower Relations from Nixon to Reagan* (Random House, 1987, pp. 147, 151). This book provided additional insight into the "Halloween Massacre" of 1975, as well as the account of the Carter campaign's "greatest fear" of a passing of a SALT agreement.

One of the key sources detailing Rumsfeld's accomplishments as secretary of defense from 1975 to 1977 was Marvin Zim's profile of Rumsfeld, *Princeton Alumni Weekly*, November 21, 2001, p. 16.

"What I learned about crisis management and troubleshooting...." Thomas M. Chesser, "It Was Tough Medicine, but G. D. Searle Breathes Easier Now," *New York Times*, January 31, 1982, III, 6:3.

Much of the background on Rumsfeld at Searle and the story of Searle suing the FDA to get approval of NutraSweet appeared in Joseph McCann's *Sweet Success* and was corroborated by *Fortune* magazine in an article entitled "Sweet Tooth," July 26, 1982, p. 30.

Rumsfeld as an "axman." Chesser, "It Was Tough Medicine, but G. D. Searle Breathes Easier Now," *New York Times*, January 31, 1982, III, 6:3.

Michael T. Klare, "Rumsfeld: Star Warrior Returns," *The Nation*, January 29, 2001, p. 15. This article included the quote from Mr. Klare on how "Bush and Rumsfeld will push much harder" for deployment of missile defense and weapons in space. It also included material on Dole attacking Clinton on his dealings with Iraq.

The background on the 1998 letter sent by Rumsfeld to President Clinton that included the request for "a strategy for removing Saddam's [Hussein] regime from power." "1998 Letter on Iraq," *New York Times*, December 3, 2001, p. A9.

The account of Rumsfeld's stance on missile defense was compiled from a variety of sources, including Klare, "Rumsfeld: Star Warrior Returns," *The Nation*, January 29, 2001, p. 14.

One key source for the information regarding the Space Commission was Michael Krepon's piece "Lost in Space: The Misguided Drive Toward Antisatellite Weapons," *Foreign Affairs*, May/June 2001, pp. 2–8.

"the weaponization of space, sooner rather than later." Mike Moore, *Bulletin of the Atomic Scientists*, March/April 2001, p. 17.

The source for the meeting between Bush and Rumsfeld in May of 1999 was Bradley Graham, *Hit to Kill*, (New York, Public Affairs, 2001), p. 343.

"The ex-CEO of G. D. Searle & Co. had bold plans...." Stan Crock, edited by Richard S. Dunham, "Why the Hawks Are Carpet-Bombing Rumsfeld," *Business Week*, August 6, 2001, p. 37.

"Rumsfeld and [Paul] O'Neill are the latest chiefs to fumble...." Fareed Zakaria, "The Myth of the Super-CEO," *Newsweek*, September 3, 2001, p. 33.

"What the uniformed guys put in place..." was excerpted from a lengthy *Time* magazine piece by Michael Duffy with additional reporting from James Carney, entitled "Rumsfeld: Older, but Wiser?," August 27, 2001, pp. 22–26.

"Plan backwards as well as forward...." Donald Rumsfeld, *Rumsfeld's Rules*, first edition, December 1, 1974, copyright 1980, revised 2001.

"*Rumsfeld's Rules* can be profitably read in any organization...." *New York Times*, December 5, 1988.

"...skilled full-time politician-bureaucrat in whom ambition, ability, and substance fuse seamlessly." Henry

Kissinger, *Years of Renewal* (New York: Simon & Schuster, 1999, p. 175).

"There is an inevitable conflict..." Dr. Henry Kissinger, interview with the author, February 19, 2002.

"I think we're dealing with Rumsfeld at a different stage..." Dr. Henry Kissinger, interview with the author, February 19, 2002.

"...ruthless within the rules." Hartmann, *Palace Politics*, p. 283.

"If you asked a seriously competent CEO...." Michael Lewis, "Odd Man In," *New York Times Magazine* (cover story), January 13, 2002.

"One source that Rumsfeld has turned to...is the groundbreaking, 1997 book by H.R. McMaster, *Dereliction of Duty....*" The influence of the book on Donald Rumsfeld and his approach to the war was detailed in a cover story by Mark Mazzetti and Richard J. Newman, "Rumsfeld's Way," in *U.S. News & World Report*, December 17, 2001, pp. 24–25.

"The greatest foreign policy disaster of the twentieth century...." H. R. McMaster, *Dereliction of Duty: Lyndon Johnson, Robert McNamara, The Joint Chiefs of Staff, and the Lies that Led to Vietnam* (New York: HarperCollins, 1997, from the introduction).

Chapter 3

"Once you allow the coalition to determine the mission...." Donald Rumsfeld, interview with *Parade* magazine, October 12, 2001.

The source for some of the background material that appears under the heading "Sidelining Haig" was James Cannon, *Time and Change: Gerald Ford's Appointment with History.* (New York: Harper-Collins, 1994, pp. 353–357.)

"When you're dealing with the immediate all the time...."
Donald Rumsfeld, interview with Georgie Anne Geyer,
October 17, 2001.

"[Another] similarity in business and government...." "A
Politician Turned Executive Surveys Both Worlds,"
Fortune, September 10, 1979, p. 88.

"In business, although it is more responsive than government....," "A Politician Turned Executive Surveys Both
Worlds," *Fortune*, September 10, 1979, p. 88.

"What we did, essentially, was tidy up some of the
pieces...." "A Politician Turned Executive Surveys Both
Worlds," *Fortune*, September 10, 1979, p. 88.

"We are, in a sense, seeing the definition of a new battlefield...." Donald Rumsfeld, Pentagon briefing, September
12, 2001.

Chapter 4

"He became the Pentagon's answer to Harry Truman...."
Mazzetti and Newman, "Rumsfeld's Way," *U.S. News
& World Report*, December 17, 2001, p. 20.

"The question is, how close we are to finding Osama bin
Laden...." Donald Rumsfeld, address to men and
women of Fort Bragg, November 21, 2001.

"Sheer intelligence, combined with the will to use it merci-
lessly,..." "Ten Toughest Bosses," *Fortune*, April 21,
1980, p. 64.

"His work as a Congressman, Secretary of Defense, and
chief of staff..." "Ten Toughest Bosses," *Fortune*, April
21, 1980, p. 62.

The story of the secret service agent was secured in an
interview with author, January 8, 2002. The agent spoke
on condition of anonymity.

Searle executive told to lose weight or risk $10,000 of his
bonus: Sally Saville Hodge, "Rumsfeld's Option: Politics

or Business," *Chicago Tribune*, July 19, 1985, Chicagoland edition, p. 2.

"According to former employees, [this CEO] conducts meetings so aggressively...." "The Toughest Bosses in America," *Fortune*, August 6, 1984, p. 18.

"You not only let someone who has not been obeying you go..." "Ten Toughest Bosses," *Fortune*, April 21, 1980, pp. 62-65.

"Unless you're a Mozart, Einstein or Mary Lou Retton....," John A. Byrne, "The New Pathfinders," *Forbes*, September 10, 1984, p. 184.

"Do you think we have a few months of long, bloody battle?" Tim Russert interview with Donald Rumsfeld on NBC's "Meet the Press," December 2, 2001.

"I am very blunt; I'm very outspoken...." Donald Rumsfeld, *Washington Post*, December 7, 2001.

Chapter 5

"Fortune often favors those that..." Hartmann, *Palace Politics*, p. 273.

"I don't consider being ruthless incompatible..." Dr. Henry Kissinger, interview with the author, February 19, 2002.

"Everything in Rummy's life seemed to come early and easily..." Hartmann, *Palace Politics*, p. 274.

"I once asked him, half in fun, if his ambition was to be president...." Robert Hartmann, *Palace Politics*, p. 274.

"This is chess, not checkers..." Bob Woodward and Dan Balz, "Combating Terrorism: 'It Starts Today,'" *Washington Post*, February 1, 2001, p. A01.

"There are always risks, but I am used to risks...." Donald Rumsfeld, "A Politician Turned Executive Surveys Both Worlds," *Fortune*, September 10, 1979, p. 90.

"After three terms he joined the Nixon administration...." David Montgomery, "The Best Defense," *Washington Post*, December 12, 2001.

"I'm not the guy to do it..." Ford, *A Time to Heal*, p. 186.

"It won't work...." Ford, *A Time to Heal*, p. 186.

Rumsfeld "was right. Everyone wanted a portion of my time...." Ibid.

"He could set the stage, pamper the star, Jerry Ford...." Clark Mollenhoff, *The Man who Pardoned Nixon*, St. Martin's Press, 1976, p. 229.

"Within ten and a half months..." Mollenhoff, *The Man who Pardoned Nixon*, p. 230.

"Above all, he was a superior administrator...." Ford, *A Time to Heal*, p. 130.

"Rumsfeld had an enormous advantage...." Hartmann, *Palace Politics*, p. 200.

"I work long hours and seven days a week...." Donald Rumsfeld, interview, *Washington Post*, December 7, 2001.

Chapter 6

"Mr. Rumsfeld...also seems to be the prime shaper of the modern, flexible sort of alliance that America is trying to assemble...," *The Economist*, October 13, 2001, p. 58.

"This war will not be waged by a grand alliance united for a single purpose of defeating an axis of hostile powers...," excerpted from an opinion piece by Donald H. Rumsfeld, *New York Times*, September 27, 2001.

"One Thursday in 1964...the future opened up...." Wil S. Hylton, "Dick and Don Go to War," *Esquire*, February 2002, pp. 83–84.

"It wasn't personal...It was about youth and power and the bare-naked fact...." ibid., pp. 83–84.

"His approach and working style [are] reflected in this organization." Hartmann, *Palace Politics*, p. 280.

"Can you tell us whose authority has been enhanced and whose authority has been diminished?" and following question and answer exchange. Hartmann, *Palace Politics*, p. 280.

"If not the hero, he was definitely the victor...." Mollenhoff, *The Man who Pardoned Nixon*, p. 229.

"There was almost no higher for Rumsfeld to go..." Wil Hylton, "Dick and Don Go to War," *Esquire*, February 2002, p. 84.

"It was just a recognition that one person has only one head...." Janet Key, "Rumsfeld turns Searle around with bottom-line management," *Chicago Tribune*, April 1, 1981.

"[Rumsfeld's] willingness to consult broadly across the firm,..." McCann, *Sweet Success*, p. 41.

"This is not...just America's fight....This is the world's fight...." President George W. Bush, address to a joint session of Congress and the American people, September 20, 2001.

"Another key turning point was the decision that we would not have a single coalition...." Donald Rumsfeld, interview, *Washington Post*, December 7, 2001.

Chapter 7

"We need to strengthen our ties to democratic allies and to challenge regimes hostile to our interests and values..," from "The Project for a New American Century," signed by Rumsfeld and others. This also appeared in Lawrence F. Kaplan's piece entitled "Containment," *The New Republic* (Online), January 26, 2001.

"We'll clean up the mess, and then the ball will be in your court..."Dan Balz and Bob Woodward, "America's Chaotic Road to War," *Washington Post*, January 27, 2002. First in a series, p. A01.

"When military decisions were brought to him... "Inside the War Room," *Time*, January 29, 2002, p. 116.

"Don't do anything that you would not like to see on the front page of the *Washington Post*." *Rumsfeld's Rules*, p. 6.

"A challenge to strive to put into practice...." Donald Rumsfeld, "Values Have Consequences," speech given at the Ethics and Public Policy Center in Washington, D.C., November 20, 1985.

"The day we lose sight of the distinction between freedom and the denial of freedom...." Ibid.

"Most Americans...became Americans because of an idea...." Ibid.

"Rumsfeld chewed my ass for smearing innocent people...." Nessen, *It Sure Looks Different from the Inside.* (Chicago: Playboy Press.) p. 31.

"We have two choices...." Donald Rumsfeld, Address to the Men and Women of Whiteman Air Force Base, October 19, 2001.

"The terrorists who visited this violence on America have made a terrible mistake...." Ibid.

"Is it possible at some point that a civilian was killed?" Donald Rumsfeld, DOD news briefing, December 27, 2001.

"We live in an age of paradoxes...." Secretary of Defense Rumsfeld, Annual Defense Department Report to Congress on the 1977 fiscal year budget, January 27, 1976.

Chapter 8

"When I took this job I had a visit with the president shortly thereafter," Donald Rumsfeld, interview with *Time* Magazine, December 31, 2001.

"I had said at an 8:00 breakfast that sometime...." Donald Rumsfeld, "Larry King Live", December 5, 2001.

"He had done what soldiers have to do..." "Old Hawk Learns New Tricks," *The Economist*, October 13, 2001, p. 58.

"...He [Rumsfeld] raised the defense-signaling U.S. offensive-readiness...." Bob Woodward and Dan Balz, *Washington Post*, "America's Chaotic Road to War," January 27, 2002: part 1 in a series, p. A01.

"Military strategy of the war..." Dr. Henry Kissinger, interview with the author, February 19, 2002.

"You can thus measure Bush as a wartime President by one simple criteria...." Edward Luttwak, "How Bush Rates," *Time*, December 31, 2001, p. 123.

"The state of change that we see in our military world...." Donald Rumsfeld, official welcoming ceremony, The Pentagon, January 26, 2001.

"I left no doubt in his mind...." Bob Woodward and Dan Balz, *We Will Rally the World*, *Washington Post*, January 28, 2002, page A01. Second in a series.

"Some people believe that the first casualty of any war is the truth...." Donald Rumsfeld, Op-Ed, *New York Times*, January 27, 2001.

"This is not a war against an individual, a group, a religion or a country...." Ibid.

"Forget about 'exit strategies'; we're looking at a sustained engagement...." Ibid.

"The task of vanquishing these terrible enemies...." Donald Rumsfeld, address to U.S. Armed Forces, September 12, 2001.

"You're part of an organization that requires you to prove yourselves..." Donald Rumsfeld, address to the Men and Women of Fort Bragg/Pope Air Force Base, November 21, 2001.

"I think his performance..." Dr. Henry Kissinger, interview with the author, February 19, 2002.

"It is critical how we define goals at the start..." Bob Woodward and Dan Balz, "We Will Rally the World," *Washington Post*, January 28, 2002, page A01. Second in a series.

"Our interest is in working with other countries...." Donald Rumsfeld, interview with Muhammad Ashraf Azim, Pakistani TV, January 29, 2002.

Chapter 9

"In any large organization, there is always the need to reach down and know how things are really functioning....," A Politician Turned Executive Surveys Both Worlds, *Fortune*, September 10, 1979, p. 91.

"When taking over a troubled company, a knowledgeable CEO checks his or her teeth to tail ratio, as they say in the military..." excerpted from a Donald Rumsfeld speech given to the House Committee on Government Management, Information and Technology, entitled "Downsizing Government," June 6, 1995.

A substantial portion of the material about Rumsfeld's decisions at Searle, such as the hiring of a new management team and the instituting of a "bad news policy," came from McCann, *Sweet Success*.

"'What I was looking for, was something outside of Washington...'" Chesser, "It Was Tough Medicine, but G. D. Searle Breathes Easier Now," *New York Times*, January 31, 1982, III, 6:3.

"I decided to do it, starting in June...." "A Politician Turned Executive Surveys Both Worlds," *Fortune*, September 10, 1979, p. 88.

"It's always been my philosophy to hire the best...." Chesser, "It Was Tough Medicine, but G. D. Searle Breathes Easier Now," *New York Times*, January 31, 1982, III, 6:3.

"Rigorous documentation and research protocols were instituted...." McCann, *Sweet Success*, p. 43.

"New financial controls and information systems had been introduced...." McCann, *Sweet Success*, p. 43.

"He forced each division to adhere to rigorous control mechanisms...." Chesser, "It Was Tough Medicine, but G.D. Searle Breathes Easier Now," *New York Times*, January 31, 1982, III, 6:3.

"We continue to conduct intelligence-gathering operations...." Donald Rumsfeld, DOD news briefing, January 11, 2001.

"And towards that end, it is of great urgency...." Ibid.

The Rumsfeld exchange with reporters on the subject of intelligence gathering and the situation in Singapore was excerpted from a DOD news briefing, January 13, 2001.

Chapter 10

"It is useful to ask whether you are working off your 'in' basket...," A Politician Turned Executive Surveys Both Worlds, *Fortune* agazine, September 10, 1979, p. 91.

"In the grand sweep of history, great leadership has always been strategic..." Donald Rumsfeld speech to the Heritage Foundation, "Strategic Imperatives in East Asia," May 15, 1988.

"The essential quality of leadership is the courage to decide...." Donald Rumsfeld, "Values Have Consequences."

"The result has been an about-face at the once ailing, overextended, and family-run company." Janet Key, "Rumsfeld Turns Searle around with Bottom-Line Management," *Chicago Tribune*, April 1, 1981.

"The first task is to decide what the core business is...." Donald Rumsfeld, "Downsizing Government," speech delivered to the House Committee on Government

Reform and Oversight, Subcommittee on Government Management, Information and Technology in Washington, D.C., on June 6, 1995.

"At home, uncertainty leads to confusion...." Donald Rumsfeld, "Strategic Imperatives in East Asia," speech to Heritage Foundation, March 3, 1998.

"President Bush takes office with three goals..." Donald Rumsfeld, official welcoming ceremony, January 26, 2001.

"Reaching those [President Bush's] goals is a matter of mission and of mindset...." Ibid.

"There was discussion of boots on the ground...." "Inside the War Room," *Time*, December 31, 2001, p. 117.

Chapter 11

"When I took over [Searle]... I was asked to be chief executive officer and run the company...," "A Politician Turned Executive Surveys Both Worlds," *Fortune*, September 10, 1979, p. 94

"I guess I'm kind of old-fashioned. I'm inclined to think that if you're going to cock it, you throw it...," Donald Rumsfeld, DOD briefing, September 12, 2001.

"What we need to do is see if we can't get arranged in a way...." Donald Rumsfeld, appearance on "Online NewsHour with Jim Lehrer," May 25, 2001.

"It's been a process of trying to,...." Donald Rumsfeld, interview with *New York Times* Editorial Board, November 14, 2001.

"You might ask, do you get so bureaucratized that you forget...." "A Politician Turned Executive Surveys Both Worlds," *Fortune*, September 10, 1979, pp. 92, 94.

"Rumsfeld, with a Resume to Rival that of Bush..." Headline, *Wall Street Journal*, May 30, 1986, p. 62.

"Brimming with self-confidence, Mr. Rumsfeld is a man who relishes a challenge..." Robert W. Merry, Rumsfeld,

With a Resume to Rival that of Bush, Prepares to Seek GOP Nomination for President," *Wall Street Journal*, May 30, 1986, pp. 62-63.

"I came to believe that if he ever reached the presidency, he might be a more comfortable chief executive...." Kissinger, *Years of Renewal*, p. 177.

"Rumsfeld Decides Against Seeking GOP Nomination," headline, *Wall Street Journal*, April 3, 1987, 3; 4.

"For a dark horse, the improbable balance...." Ibid.

"...regretted when he withdrew..." Dr. Henry Kissinger, interview with the author, February 19, 2002.

"Had the reason for his tenacious procrastination all along been a congenital dread of a setback...?" Kissinger, *Years of Renewal*, p. 177.

"A man with a job like his needs two connected qualities...." "Old Hawk Learns New Tricks," *The Economist*, October 13, 2001, p. 58.

"...that the first 36 hours of the crisis..." Bob Woodward and Dan Balz, "We Will Rally the World," *Washington Post*, January 28, 2002, page A01. Second in a series.

Chapter 12

"...You must attack. The only way to deal with terrorists is to take it to them. And that must be done...," Donald Rumsfeld interview with Georgie Anne Geyer, October 17, 2001.

"What do we mean by victory? Victory means liquidating the terrorist networks and putting them out of business...," Donald Rumsfeld, Address to the Men and Women of Whiteman Air Force Base, October 19, 2001.

The section entitled "What to do when backed into a corner," which features Rumsfeld's battle with the FDA, was the subject of *Sweet Success*, by Joseph McCann.

Much of the background material for this section came from that book.

"If there was ever a single moment...." Bradley Graham, *Hit to Kill: The Battle Over Shielding America from Missile Attack*, New York: Public Affairs, 2001, p. 31.

"By speaking in a unanimous voice...." Ibid, p. 47.

"There have been people making those kinds of arguments...." Donald Rumsfeld, interview on "CNN Late Edition," September 9, 2001.

"There is not likely to be any single, simple 'doctrine'...." Donald Rumsfeld, *Strategic Imperatives in East Asia*, speech delivered to B.C. Lee Lecture, Heritage Foundation, Washington, D.C., March 3, 1998.

"We need to recognize that it's unlikely that armies...." Donald Rumsfeld, "We Are Vigilant," *Newsweek*, December 24, 2001.

"Rumsfeld appears to hold special honors..." Jeffrey Gedmin, "Meet Mr. Rumsfeld," *Wall Street Journal*, European edition, May 23, 2001.

"The study warns that the United States may someday soon...." Michael Krepon, "Lost in Space: The Misguided Drive Toward Antisatellite Weapons," *Foreign Affairs*, May/June, 2001, pp. 2–7.

"Stay out of the heavens," opinion piece that claimed that "the United States should not race against itself," Michael E. O'Hanlon, Op-Ed,*Chicago Tribune*, May 21, 2001.

"I never bought the criticism that somehow he was a relic of the past." Dick Cheney, in interview with Chief White House Correspondent Kenneth T. Walsh, *U.S. News & World Report*, December 17, 2001, p. 25.

"There is absolutely no doubt that..." Dr. Henry Kissinger, interview with the author, February 19, 2002.

The "Axis of Evil"

"Concerted efforts by a number of overtly or potentially hostile nations..." *Executive Summary of the Report of the Commission to Assess the Ballistic Missile Threat to the United States*, July 15, 1998, Pursuant to Public Law 201, 104th Congress, p. 3.

"A world with six billion people will not be led into a peaceful future..." Steven Erlanger [in Berlin], "Europe Steps Up Attacks on Bush," *The New York Times*, February 14, 2001.

"The extraordinary level of resources North Korea and Iran..", *Executive Summary of the Report of the Commission to Assess the Ballistic Missile Threat to the United States*, p. 6.

"...the latest evidence of why he is precisely the Defense Secretary the nation needs..." *Wall Street Journal*, Editorial Page, January 12, 2001.

"Powell says U.S. is Weighing Ways to Topple Hussein," *The New York Times* [headline], February 13, 2002, page 1, column 1.

"To the extent that the Rumsfeld..." Dr. Henry Kissinger, interview with the author, February 19, 2002.

"Time is not on our side. I will not wait on events..." President George W. Bush, State of the Union Address, January 29, 2001.

INDEX